The Generic Challenge

The Generic Challenge:

Understanding Patents, FDA and Pharmaceutical Life-Cycle Management
Fourth Edition

Martin A. Voet, B.S., M.B.A., J.D.

BrownWalker Press
Boca Raton

The Generic Challenge:
Understanding Patents, FDA and Pharmaceutical Life-Cycle Management
(Fourth Edition)

Cover image by mirceab/Bigstock.com

BrownWalker Press
Boca Raton, Florida • USA
2014
www.brownwalker.com

ISBN-10: 1-61233-728-7
ISBN-13: 978-1-61233-728-9

Library of Congress Cataloging-in-Publication Data

Voet, Martin A., 1942-
The Generic Challenge : Understanding Patents, FDA and Pharmaceutical Life-Cycle Management / Martin A. Voet. – 4th Ed.
    p. ; cm.
    ISBN-13: 978-1-61233-728-9 (pbk. :alk. paper)
    ISBN-10: 1-61233-728-7 (pbk. :alk. paper)
1. Drugs–Generic substitution–Law and legislation–United States.
2. Drugs–United States–Generic substitution–Patents. 3. Patent extensions–United States. 4. Pharmaceutical biotechnology–Patents. 5. Pharmaceutical biotechnology–Law and legislation. I. Title.

[DNLM: 1. Drugs, Generic–economics–United States. 2. Legislation, Drug–United States. 3. Drug Industry–economics–United States. 4. Drug Industry–legislation & jurisprudence–United States. 5. Patents as Topic–legislation & jurisprudence–United States. QV 33 AA1 V876g 2008]

KF3894.G45V64 2008
346.7304'86–dc22

                                                            2008003218

Dedication

In Greek mythology, Cassandra was the astonishly beautiful daughter of King Priam and Queen Hecuba of Troy. Her great beauty caused the God Apollo to grant her the gift of foreseeing the future. But when Cassandra refused Apollo's attempted seduction, he placed a curse on her that her predictions of the future, as well as the predictions of all her descendants, while true, would not be believed.

I would like to dedicate this Fourth Edition to my good and wise friend and colleague, George Lasezkay, a likely descendant of Cassandra.

*"The desire to take medicine is perhaps
the greatest feature which distinguishes man from animals"*
Sir William Osler, M.D.

Contents

Disclaimer

This book is intended to provide information about the subject matter covered. It is sold with the understanding that the publisher and author are not engaged in rendering legal services or providing legal advice. If legal advice is required, the services of a competent legal adviser should be obtained.

Reasonable efforts have been made to make this book accurate and complete. However, there may be mistakes, both typographical and in content. Therefore, this text should be used only as a general guide and is not to be relied on in any particular, keeping in mind that laws and interpretation of rules change over time.

The purpose of this book is to educate and inform. The author and publisher shall have neither liability nor responsibility to any person or entity with respect to any loss or damage caused or alleged to be caused directly or indirectly by the information contained in this book.

The opinions expressed in this book are solely the personal opinions of the author in his individual capacity. Nothing in this book shall be attributable to the author in any representational capacity or to any other person or legal entity.

Acknowledgments

I have not attempted to cite in the text all of the authorities and sources consulted in the preparation of this book. To do so would make the book cumbersome and probably unreadable to the non-professional. Besides, I wanted to write an enjoyable book that would be easy to read and understand and by implication, that means no footnotes.

Thanks to friends and colleagues for offering suggestions and improvements; and to Matthea Cohen for editing and especially to my good friend and colleague, George Lasezkay, for encouraging me to write this book, whose genesis was a chapter outline sketched out on a yellow legal pad in the spring sunshine of Sun Valley, Idaho between ski runs on Baldy.

About the Author

Martin A. Voet was formerly Senior Vice President and Chief Intellectual Property Counsel for a Fortune 500 pharmaceutical company with over twenty-five years' experience in pharmaceutical intellectual property practice. He is currently a consultant in intellectual property management and pharmaceutical product exclusivity and Adjunct Professor of Law at the University of San Diego Law School.

He graduated from the University of California at Berkeley with a B.S. degree in Chemistry; received an M.B.A. degree from Pepperdine University School of Business and Management and was awarded a J.D. Degree with Honors from the George Washington University National Law Center. He is a member of the State Bar of California.

He has been a contributor to the Practicing Law Institute's *Global Intellectual Property* Series and its annual *Patent Litigation* series. He was also a contributor and member of the Editorial Board of *Managing Intellectual Property*. He has been a speaker at ACI's annual *Maximizing Pharmaceutical Patent Life Cycles* in New York and co-chaired ACI's West Coast conference on *Paragraph IV Disputes*.

Preface to the Fourth Edition

For the first time in the last 50 years, the cost for pharmaceutical drugs in the U.S. has actually declined. In 2012, the rise of generics cut the nation's tab for prescription medications by 1% to $325.8 billion or $898 per person according to IMS Health. The main reason for this new phenomenon was a number of very popular and effective medicines losing patent protection and being replaced by inexpensive generics.

Since the writing of the first edition ten years ago, the generic industry has continued to grow stronger at the expense of the innovative pharmaceutical industry. According to IMS Health, the percentage market share for brands vs generics in the U.S. has dramatically declined to only 20.4% in 2012.

But the brand drug companies are fighting back. New FDA drug approvals on innovative drugs have significantly increased from 21 approved in 2010 to 39 approved in 2012, though there were also 152 first time generic approvals that same year. Nonetheless, the future does not look bright for the brand drug industry. Evaluate Pharma estimates that 15 key patent expirations in 2013 will result in $29 billion in Rx branded drug sales becoming generic and as much as $290 billion between 2013 and 2018.

Who do you think is the country's biggest supplier of prescription drugs? Is it J&J or Pfizer in the U.S. or GlaxoSmithKline in the U.K., or Roche or Novartis in Switzerland? No. It is Teva Pharmaceuticals, a generic manufacturer based in Israel with annual revenues of $20 billion. Teva says it is responsible for one of every six prescriptions filled in the U.S.

At the same time, annual fees that branded prescription drug companies must pay FDA are going up. For example, for fiscal 2013, under the Prescription Drug User Fee Act (PDUFA), a fee of $2.2 million is required for each new brand drug filing, up from $1.4 million in 2010. But generics must pay now as well. Under the Generic Drug User Fee Amendments of 2012, the FDA plans to raise $300 million in funding for fiscal 2013 by charging filing fees to generic companies, including a onetime ANDA backlog fee.

Generic drug filings and approvals have continued to increase, though success has produced some growing pains. FDA's Office of Generic Drugs (OGD) reported recently that its backlog of new ANDA filings awaiting approval is nearing 3,000, triple the backlog from 2005, and its median ANDA approval time was 31 months for fiscal 2013, up from 16 months in 2005.

Unless the foregoing is remedied, it may have some unintended consequences for the generic drug industry. One of the requirements to avoid forfeiture of the much coveted 180-day exclusivity provided to "first-filer" generics by the **Hatch Waxman Act** is to be approved within 30 months of filing an ANDA. If FDA cannot get a first-filer generic drug approved within 30 months of filing, that generic would lose its 180-day exclusivity. FDA recognizes this problem and has said it is trying to avoid that outcome by giving preference to first filers.

On March 23, 2010, President Obama signed into law healthcare reform legislation officially known as the "**Patient Protection and Affordable Care Act**", and unofficially known as "Obamacare". This legislation contains provisions establishing for the first time an abbreviated regulatory pathway for generic versions of biologically produced medicines called "biosimilars". Chapter seven covers the new law and its implications for the biotech drug industry, as well as highlights of recently published FDA regulations for biosimilars.

This same law also provides for additional tax revenue from the branded prescription drug industry in the form of an annual excise tax starting in 2011 of $2.5 billion and peaking at $4 billion annually in 2018. And there is a new 2.3% excise tax due from manufacturers and importers on sales of most medical devices. Let's hope they all remain healthy enough to continue to pay these new taxes.

It is also my hope this Fourth Edition will be a useful update of the book as the laws and regulations and court decisions affecting this fascinating subject continue to evolve.

Martin A. Voet
October 1, 2013

Preface to the First Edition

A horse walks into a bar and the bartender says, "Why the long face?" Why indeed. The pharmaceutical industry should be on top of the world with innovative discoveries and development of so many fantastic new drugs for treating life-threatening illnesses, while often avoiding expensive surgeries. There are targeted new drugs for treating once deadly cancers and for preventing blindness; wondrous new life-saving biotech products for treating stroke and multiple sclerosis; amazing new lifestyle enhancement drugs from growing hair and erasing wrinkles to maintaining sexual vigor; yet the pharmaceutical industry is trashed nightly as being second only to the tobacco industry in the corporations-we-hate-most department.

Politicians sensing this are quick to lay blame, announce conspiracies, demand lower prices and push for re-importation of low-priced drugs from foreign countries. African countries blame them as if they started the AIDS epidemic, instead of coming up with promising treatments. Generic drugs are thought to be the answer to what is wrong with healthcare, while innovators are viewed at best with a jaundiced eye. In this charged and decidedly unfriendly environment, why write this book?

In fact there is nothing wrong with generics and they are a valuable and necessary part of a good health care system. However, there would be no generics without the innovators and I am worried that the public has lost sight of this truism. This book is intended to encourage the innovators to persevere in the face of this adversity and to redouble their efforts to innovate and to continue to see themselves as the valuable contributors to society that they are.

Martin A. Voet
December 3, 2004

Introduction

The Generic Challenge is about providing the necessary information to pharmaceutical executives, managers, regulatory, legal and business development professionals, those involved in strategic marketing and in research and development, among others in the pharmaceutical field, to deal with the increasingly aggressive tactics of generic companies designed to legally copy innovative drug products.

Generic drugs offer significant benefits to society by providing good, low cost medicines at affordable prices. But people and their children also will need new and better innovative drugs in the future to treat a variety of unmet needs. If the generic industry is not kept in check, the balance between the goals of low-priced currently available drugs and innovative, life-saving and life-enhancing *future* drugs will not be maintained, and while we will continue to have available inexpensive older generic drugs, we will have fewer new, innovative drugs.

Most people don't understand that new, innovative drugs are invented and developed by the drug industry without any significant help from the government. Sometimes the basic concepts are discovered at Universities and are licensed to the pharmaceutical companies at a very early stage in development, and once in a while something comes from a government-sponsored research institute, such as the National Institutes of Health (NIH), but not very often. And even then, the long times and great costs and capital risks for development and approval by FDA are all on the pharmaceutical industry alone.

A significant percentage of the profits made by the drug companies in marketing and selling their current drugs is invested in the research needed to discover and develop future new drugs. No profits on current drugs, no research on new drugs.

Generic companies have no expense for discovery or development or marketing of drugs. They are legally allowed to copy an innovator's drug after a relatively short time of exclusivity for the innovator, unless there is patent protection. If they can overcome the patent protection, they can legally obtain rights to use all the safety and efficacy data developed by the innovator and copy the drug. Then they only have to manufacture the drug and put it on the market. No payments are due to the innovator by the generic company for use of his property.

A comparable situation would be you building a house and putting a lock on the door and then after a period of time, anyone who can pick the lock can legally use your house. Well, you say, that's not fair. I built and paid for the house, no one should be able to use it just because they can pick the lock. You are right of course. No one would dream of that kind of legal process for houses. But that is precisely what happens in the wonderful world of pharmaceuticals where a generic company gets free use of your FDA drug file if he can pick the lock of your patent. In fact, current law actually gives generic companies *an incentive* to do so by providing a period of exclusivity for the first generic company that tries to pick a product's patent lock!

In the last 30 years since the Hatch Waxman Act fostered the generics industry, it has grown steadily, so that by 2013 it accounted for 80% market share of the prescription drugs sold in America, according to IMS Health. Not satisfied with that enviable track record, during recent years, the generic drug companies have adopted a "take no prisoners" attitude and are challenging virtually all new drug patents at the earliest possible time. Branded pharmaceutical companies today have virtually all of their current products under attack by generics.

One of the main reasons for the on-going consolidation of the pharmaceutical industry is the shortening of product life-cycles caused by generics entering the market at earlier times in the product life-cycle. As the innovative product life-cycle gets shorter, simple economics suggests that the pharmaceutical industry must recover its long term investment over the shorter time period. This inevitably results in higher drug prices, which leads to further political pressures for Canadian re-importation of lower priced drugs, price controls, excise taxes on new drugs, etc.

Under such conditions, it would not be wise to take the survival of the innovative pharmaceutical industry for granted. An interesting example of this is the drug policy in Canada which has now come full circle.

The Canadian government decided many years ago that it preferred to reimburse inexpensive generic drugs to more costly innovative branded drugs and established governmental policies to achieve that. There was no data protection in Canada for drug dossiers and the only thing preventing a new pharmaceutical product becoming generic almost from day one was a patent. Even there the law was not very friendly to innovators and it was the policy of the health authorities and even the courts to officially favor the generic industry.

The net result was that there is virtually no innovative drug industry in Canada and like Blanche in *A Street Car Named Desire*; it depends on the kindness of strangers for future innovative drugs. Interestingly, because of price controls for branded drugs, innovative drugs are cheaper in Canada than in the

U.S., but generic drugs are more expensive. If all countries took Canada's approach, eventually, there would be no innovative pharmaceutical industry and no new innovative drugs.

To Canada's credit it has now recognized the negative aspects of its drug policy and has implemented new regulations to provide for up to eight years of regulatory exclusivity for new drugs approved after June 17, 2006. This will encourage innovation by insuring a minimum of eight years of exclusivity for a new drug before it can be made available in Canada as a generic drug. Further details on the new Canadian drug rules can be found in Chapters 5 and 6.

The purpose of this book is to familiarize the reader with both the strategic and tactical aspects of the interactions of patents, FDA regulations, and the **Hatch Waxman Act** and product improvements on pharmaceutical product life-cycles.

However, this is not as easy as it may sound. Patent law tends to be an arcane specialty with its own jargon like "prior art", "terminal disclaimer" and "102 reference"; while FDA law, with its dense and almost impossible to understand regulations and its own jargon like "505(b)(2) filing" and "Phase III clinical trial", is not much better.

The following Dilbert carton does a pretty good job of illustrating how many people think about patents: somehow important, but at the same time not very understandable.

Furthermore, when you need an answer to a patent question, you ask a patent lawyer. If the question also involves FDA regulatory issues, you will generally be told that that is an area outside the expertise of the patent lawyer and you should consult an expert in FDA law or regulation. So you find such a person and they will tell you all you need to know about FDA law and regulations, but if the question also involves patents in any significant way, they will tell you it is outside their area of expertise, so please to consult a patent lawyer.

This Catch 22 problem for pharmaceutical managers and executives is that there are an increasing number of important "you bet your product" issues that depend on fully understanding how patent and regulatory laws and regulations and statutes such as the Hatch Waxman Act interact to influence the long-term success of a pharmaceutical product.

That means pharmaceutical managers and executives alike who want to succeed in their jobs have no choice but to become knowledgeable in these matters, so that they can plan for the successful development and long term success of their company's pharmaceutical products. This book might also be helpful to the regulatory lawyer or patent lawyer (who can save time by skipping the chapter on his or her specialty) who wishes he or she had a better understanding of the interaction of patent law with regulatory law so that they can better see the bigger picture and help achieve the goal of successful pharmaceutical product life-cycle management.

This book is intended to explain those subjects in understandable language so that you, the reader, will be able to ask the right questions and understand the answers you receive. Keep in mind this book is not intended to be, nor could it be, a substitute for competent counsel in patent law and FDA regulatory matters, nor is it a substitute for expert consultants in pharmaceutical product life-cycle management.

The first three chapters are on patents. Chapter 1 is an **Overview of Patents**. Chapter 2 covers **Patent Enforcement**

and Infringement and Chapter 3 describes **Pharmaceutical, Biological and Medical Device Patents**. These chapters provide the necessary basic background in patents for understanding pharmaceutical product life-cycle management. The next two chapters relate to regulatory matters. Chapter 4 is an **Overview of FDA** and chapter 5 covers **Drug Product Exclusivity**. These chapters provide the basics for understanding how these regulations and the available product exclusivities affect product life-cycle management. Chapters 6 and 7 discuss the final pieces of the puzzle: for conventional drugs, the 1984 **Hatch Waxman Act**; and for biologically produced drugs, the 2010 **Patient Protection and Affordable Act** which for the first time authorizes generics for biologically produced branded drugs in the United States ("biosimilars"). Then Chapter 8 synthesizes the previous seven chapters in **Putting it All Together: Product Life-Cycle Management**. Finally Chapter 9 closes with some **Conclusions and Final Thoughts**.

Chapter 1

Overview of Patents

*"Lo, this only have I found that God hath made
man upright; but they have sought out
many inventions."*

Ecclesiastes 7:29

*The invention all admired,
and each, how he
To be the inventor missed,
so easy it seemed
Once found, which yet unfound
most would have
thought impossible.*

John Milton
Paradise Lost

WHAT IS A PATENT?

Patents have been around longer than you may think. Article I,
Section 8 of the U.S. constitution provides that

"Congress shall have the Power ... to promote the Progress of Science and **Useful Arts** *by securing for limited Times to Authors and* **Inventors** *the exclusive Right to their respective Writings and* **Discoveries***."*

As an interesting historical tidbit, President George Washington signed the first patent bill in 1790 which laid the foundations of the modern American patent system. The U.S. patent system was unique; for the first time in history the right of an inventor to profit from his invention was recognized by law. Previously, privileges granted to an inventor were dependent upon the prerogative of a monarch or upon a special act of a legislature.

In that same year, one Samuel Hopkins of Pittsford, Vermont, was granted the first U.S. patent on an improved method of making potash. The reviewer of this patent was none other than Thomas Jefferson, the then Secretary of State. Jefferson granted the patent after obtaining signatures from the Attorney General and from President Washington.

Well, enough history. Classically, a patent is often described as a legal monopoly. We will find later that this description of a patent is not so accurate. Technically, a patent is a governmental grant that provides the holder for a limited period of time the exclusive right *to prevent others* from making, using or selling the patented product or process in exchange for his disclosure of the invention to the public. The careful reader will note we did *not* say the patent granted the *owner* the right to make, use or sell the invention. That basic distinction is a hard one to understand and will be discussed further. Patents are also intended to benefit the public, as they encourage less secrecy, so that important information is not lost when its owner dies, and to provide a means to encourage capital formation and investment in new ideas resulting in new industries, jobs, etc.

Probably the most famous invention of all is the Edison patent for the electric light bulb shown on the following page, along with a standard front cover of a U.S. patent. Not only has the invention lasted for well over a hundred years, but the electric light bulb has become the icon for invention itself!

You will notice the Edison patent is fairly short, consisting of only a few pages and only four claims. These days, patents tend to be longer, some running to hundreds of pages and often including hundreds of claims, but brevity, as in some other forms of human communication, can often be wiser, and in any case less expensive, as patent lawyers are usually paid by the hour.

So now we know a patent is a time-limited right to exclude others from making, using or selling a product or process. So what is a "product" or "process"? The U.S. Supreme Court has broadly interpreted it as "anything under the sun made by man" when they agreed that the first man-made bacteria engineered to eat oil could be patented. More specifically, a "product" can be a medical device such as an artificial heart or a composition of matter, such as a new chemical compound or biological agent, such as a vaccine, or formulation for a drug product or anything manufactured including a mouse genetically engineered to get cancer. A typical pharmaceutical product would consist of a patented chemical, known as a new chemical entity (NCE) and a patentable new formulation, such as an oral or topical dosage form, for delivery of the new chemical entity to the body.

A "process" as applied to pharmaceutical products is a method of treatment of persons or materials to produce a given result. Included in patentable processes are methods of manufacturing a new chemical entity or a new method of manufacturing a known compound. A process is also a method of treating a condition or disease with either a new drug (first medical use) or an old drug that was previously known for treating a different condition or disease (second medical use).

The next sentence is the most important thing to know about patents. *A patent is a sword, not a shield.* That is, a patent is primarily an offensive weapon that allows its owner, by

The Director of the United States Patent and Trademark Office

Has received an application for a patent for a new and useful invention. The title and description of the invention are enclosed. The requirements of law have been complied with, and it has been determined that a patent on the invention shall be granted under the law.

Therefore, this

United States Patent

Grants to the person(s) having title to this patent the right to exclude others from making, using, offering for sale, or selling the invention throughout the United States of America or importing the invention into the United States of America for the term set forth below, subject to the payment of maintenance fees as provided by law.

If this application was filed prior to June 8, 1995, the term of this patent is the longer of seventeen years from the date of grant of this patent or twenty years from the earliest effective U.S. filing date of the application, subject to any statutory extension.

If this application was filed on or after June 8, 1995, the term of this patent is twenty years from the U.S. filing date, subject to any statutory extension. If the application contains a specific reference to an earlier filed application or applications under 35 U.S.C. 120, 121 or 365(c), the term of the patent is twenty years from the date on which the earliest application was filed, subject to any statutory extensions.

Director of the United States Patent and Trademark Office

1. *Cover page of a U.S. Patent*

T. A. EDISON.
Electric-Lamp.

No. 223,898.   **Patented Jan. 27, 1880.**

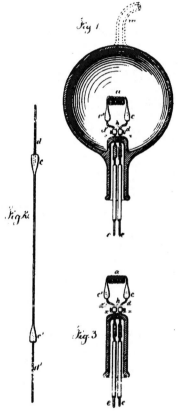

Witnesses

Chas H Smith
Geo T Pinckney

Inventor

Thomas A. Edison

for Lemuel W. Serrell

atty.

UNITED STATES PATENT OFFICE.

THOMAS A. EDISON, OF MENLO PARK, NEW JERSEY

ELECTRIC LAMP.

SPECIFICATION forming part of Letters Patent No. 223,898, dated January 27, 1880.

Application filed November 4, 1879.

To all whom it may concern:

Be it known that I, THOMAS ALVA EDISON, of Menlo Park, in the State of New Jersey, United States of America, have invented an Improvement in Electric Lamps, and in the method of manufacturing the same, (Case No. 186,) of which the following is a specification.

The object of this invention is to produce electric lamps giving light by incandescence, which lamps shall have high resistance, so as to allow of the practical subdivision of the electric light.

The invention consists in a light-giving body of carbon wire or sheets coiled or arranged in such a manner as to offer great resistance to the passage of the electric current, and at the same time present but a slight surface from which radiation can take place.

The invention further consists in placing such burner of great resistance in a nearly-perfect vacuum, to prevent oxidation and injury to the conductor by the atmosphere. The current is conducted into the vacuum-bulb through platina wires sealed into the glass.

The invention further consists in the method of manufacturing carbon conductors of high resistance, so as to be suitable for giving light by incandescence, and in the manner of securing perfect contact between the metallic conductors or leading-wires and the carbon conductor.

Heretofore light by incandescence has been obtained from rods of carbon of one to four ohms resistance, placed in closed vessels, in which the atmospheric air has been replaced by gases that do not combine chemically with the carbon. The vessel holding the burner has been composed of glass cemented to a metallic base. The connection between the leading wires and the carbon has been obtained by clamping the carbon to the metal. The leading-wires have always been large, so that their resistance shall be many times less than the burner, and, in general, the attempts of previous persons have been to reduce the resistance of the carbon rod. The disadvantages of following this practice are, that a lamp having but one to four ohms resistance cannot be worked in great numbers in multiple arc without the employment of main conductors of enormous dimensions; that, owing to the low resistance of the lamp, the leading-wires must be of large

dimensions and good conductors, and a glass globe cannot be kept tight at the place where the wires pass in and are cemented; hence the most a perfect vacuum to render the carbon stable, especially when such carbon is small in mass and high in electrical resistance.

The use of a gas in the receiver at the atmospheric pressure, although not attacking the carbon, serves to destroy it in time by "air-washing," or the attrition produced by the rapid passage of the air over the slightly-coherent highly-heated surface of the carbon. I have reversed this in practice. I have discovered that even a cotton thread properly carbonized and placed in a sealed glass bulb exhausted to one-millionth of an atmosphere offers from one hundred to five hundred ohms resistance to the passage of the current, and that it is absolutely stable at very high temperatures; that if the thread be coiled as a spiral and carbonized, or if any fibrous vegetable substance which will leave a carbon residue after heating in a closed chamber be so coiled, as much as two thousand ohms resistance may be obtained without presenting a radiating-surface greater than three-sixteenths of an inch; that if such fibrous material be rubbed with a plastic composed of lamp-black and tar, its resistance may be made high or low, according to the amount of lamp-black placed upon it; that carbon filaments may be made by a combination of tar and lamp-black, the latter being previously ignited in a closed crucible for several hours and afterward moistened and kneaded until it assumes the consistency of thick putty. Small pieces of this material may be rolled out in the form of wire as small as seven one-thousandths of a inch in diameter and over a foot in length, and the same may be covered with a non-conducting non-carbonizing substance and wound on a bobbin, or as a spiral, and the tar carbonized in a closed chamber by subjecting it to high heat, the spiral after carbonization retaining its form.

All these forms are fragile and cannot be clamped to the leading wires with sufficient force to insure good contact and prevent heating. I have discovered that if platinum wires are used and the plastic lamp-black and tar material be molded around it in the act of carbonization there is an intimate union by com-

2 **233,898**

material be molded around it in the act of carbonization there is an intimate union by combination and by pressure between the carbon and platina, and nearly perfect contact is obtained without the necessity of clamps; hence the burner and the leading-wires are connected to the carbon ready to be placed in the vacuum-bulb.

When fibrous material is used the plastic lamp-black and tar are used to secure it to the platina before carbonizing.

By using the carbon wire of such high resistance I am enabled to use fine platinum wires for leading-wires, as they will have a small resistance compared to the burner, and hence will not heat and crack the sealed vacuum-bulb. Platina can only be used, as its expansion is nearly the same as that of glass.

By using a considerable length of carbon wire and coiling it the exterior, which is only a small portion of its entire surface, will form the principal radiating-surface; hence I am able to raise the specific heat of the whole of the carbon, and thus prevent the rapid reception and disappearance of the light, which on a plain wire is prejudicial, as it shows the least unsteadiness of the current by the flickering of the light; but if the current is steady the defect does not show.

I have carbonized and used cotton and linen thread, wood splints, papers coiled in various ways, also lamp-black, plumbago, and carbon in various forms, mixed with tar and kneaded so that the same may be rolled out into wires of various lengths and diameters. Each wire, however, is to be uniform in size throughout.

If the carbon thread is liable to be distorted during carbonization it is to be coiled between a helix of copper wire. The ends of the carbon or filament are secured to the platina leading-wires by plastic carbonizable material, and the whole placed in the carbonizing-chamber. The copper, which has served to prevent distortion of the carbon thread, is afterward eaten away by nitric acid, and the spiral soaked in water, and then dried and placed on the glass holder, and a glass bulb blown over the whole, with a leading-tube for exhaustion by a mercury-pump. This tube, when a high

vacuum has been reached, is hermetically sealed.

With substances which are not greatly distorted in carbonizing, they may be coated with a non-conducting non-carbonizable substance, which allows one coil or turn of the carbon to rest upon and be supported by the other.

In the drawings, Figure 1 shows the lamp. *c c'* are the thickened ends of the spiral, formed of the plastic compound of lamp-black and tar. *d d'* are the platina wires. *h h* are the clamps, which serve to connect the platina wires, cemented in the carbon, with the leading-wires *x x*, sealed in the glass vacuum-bulb. *e e* are copper wires, connected just outside the bulb to the wires *x x*. *m* is the tube (shown by dotted lines) leading to the vacuum-pump, which, after exhaustion, is hermetically sealed and the surplus removed.

Fig. 2 represents the plastic material before being wound into a spiral.

Fig. 3 shows the spiral after carbonization, ready to have a bulb blown over it.

I claim as my invention—

1. An electric lamp for giving light by incandescence, consisting of a filament of carbon of high resistance, made as described, and secured to metallic wires, as set forth.

2. The combination of carbon filaments with a receiver made entirely of glass and conductors passing through the glass, and from which receiver the air is exhausted, for the purposes set forth.

3. A carbon filament or strip coiled and connected to electric conductors so that only a portion of the surface of such carbon conductors shall be exposed for radiating light, as set forth.

4. The method herein described of securing the platina contact-wires to the carbon filament and carbonizing of the whole in a closed chamber, substantially as set forth.

Signed by me this 1st day of November, A. D. 1879.

THOMAS A. EDISON.

Witnesses:
S. L. GRIFFIN,
JOHN F. RANDOLPH.

2. *Edison's Electric Light patent*

enforcement of the patent, to prevent others from making the patented item or using or selling the patented method during the life of the patent. However, the patent has little or no defensive character and thus *it cannot protect you from being sued for infringement* under someone else's patent. Most people find this concept the most difficult one to understand. If I have a patent on my gizmo, how can I be sued for patent infringement? The answer is simple. A patent is a sword, not a shield. As mentioned earlier, *a patent does not grant its owner the right to do anything.* Instead, it grants the owner the right to *prevent others* from doing something.

The following example may help explain this counterintuitive concept. If I owned the patent for the first carburetor, which I designed to have two barrels, and later you improved my carburetor and obtained a patent on the first 4-barrel carburetor, what happens? I can keep your 4-barrel carburetor off the market with my general patent covering carburetors, but you can prevent me from selling your 4-barrel version of my carburetor with your patent. So if we both want to sell 4-barrel carburetors, we must cross-license our patents to each other *or neither of us can make or sell them.* My broad carburetor patent does not shield me from your 4-barrel carburetor improvement patent and your improvement patent does not give you *any rights* to make or sell your improvement.

Note that this dynamic system encourages others to make improvements of your invention so they can potentially negotiate entrance into the market. This technique of patenting improvements is practiced to the point of frustration in Japan where obtaining a patent can take 5–10 years and by the time the originator has patented the basic concept, there may be 20 patents in the hands of others covering a myriad of minor improvements. As a result, the patented article is difficult to make without running into one of the improvement patents thus forcing a cross-license.

TERM OF A PATENT

In the U.S., patents used to have a term of 17 years from the date the patent was *granted*. This was set in stone. There were some exceptions, such as a shorter term caused by a terminal disclaimer (here comes that pesky jargon) where Patent Office rules require a patent owner to voluntarily agree to shorten his patent life in order to obtain the patent, but in general the rule was 17 years from date of grant. That was fair because if your patent application were held up in the Patent Office by government red tape, you would still get your 17 years once it was finally granted.

The rest of the world, on the other hand, gives 20 years from the date of *filing* the patent. This can allow quite a bit of mischief since it may take years to get the patent and any time lost in getting the patent is just hard luck for the patent owner. And competitors are happy to assist in any delays at the Patent Office through oppositions and other such procedures that allow competitors to challenge the grant of a patent. As a result it takes five to ten years to get a patent fully and finally granted in Europe and Japan, compared to one to three years in the U.S.

Then along came *harmonization*, a catchy word, but one that can lead to trouble. In the interests of harmonization, the U.S. agreed to match the other countries' rules so, effective June 8, 1995, any patents filed on or after that date had a life of 20 years from date of filing. Patents filed before that date got the longer of the two ways to compute their life (if only we all had that choice).

There was one catch and that was that the filing date the term of the patent was based on was the *earliest effective filing date* for the patent. This is because patent holders in the U.S. can file follow-on patent applications based entirely (continuations) or in part (continuations-in-part) on the former patent application and get the benefit of the date of filing of the first-filed patent application for all common subject matter. If you file a string of patent applications as continuation (CON) applications or continuations-in-part (CIP) applications, the patent life for the last patent in the string is based on the filing date of the first patent application.

Typically, a patent attorney will use a continuation application to try to get claims granted in a follow-on patent application when time for prosecution before the Patent Office has run out on the originally filed application or when only some of the claims he or she wanted were granted in the originally filed application (thus a second bite at the apple). A continuation-in-part application is typically used to add something to an already existing application, such as a new preferred formulation or some additional examples of compounds that were not disclosed in the original application.

In addition, there are complicated rules which provide for additional patent life to compensate for certain patent office delays. For example, if there were delays in prosecution caused by the U.S. Patent Office, or if you successfully appealed an Examiner's adverse ruling, the time taken for appeal will be added to your patent's life.

There are also patent term extensions available for new drug patents to compensate for delays in obtaining FDA approval. As a result, just about every patent has a different life from every other one and you can buy software to help you make sure the Patent Office calculated your patent term correctly (oh for the good old days when just about every U.S. patent had a fixed life of 17 years from date of grant).

A patent can also have a shorter term if the patent holder agrees to shorten it. For example, one might agree to this due to a legal requirement to avoid a rejection on grounds of "double patenting". This involves having more than one patent covering essentially the same invention and may be allowed only if the later filed patent expires on the same date as the earlier filed patent (the so-called "terminal disclaimer").

Also in the interests of harmonization, the U.S. joined the international community in publishing patent applications 18 months after they are filed, unless you ask not to be published *and* agree not to file the patent outside the U.S. If you recall the beginning of the chapter where the granting of a patent was a reward for *disclosure* of the invention, there seems something basically wrong with forcing the disclosure of the invention without first granting the patent! But that is now the law and the only way to get around it is to agree not to file abroad.

Submarine Patents

These new rules also solved a problem that had been invented by a man named Lemelson. Lemelson filed numerous patent applications in the 1950s on a variety of forward-thinking concepts and then he did an unusual thing. Instead of being in a hurry to get his patents granted, he took his time and re-filed the applications as continuation applications and kept adding subtle refinements to the claims and kept doing so *for 40 years* until, in the early 1990s when he finally allowed his patents to be granted, they covered important modern inventions. Since his patents were based on the old rules, he got a 17-year life from the date of grant.

After his patents were granted, he asked just about every company in the U.S. for royalties and got them after suing many. He collected over a *billion dollars* in royalties. His inventions ranged from Hot Wheels track to bar coding (the black and white bars and numbers on just about every box of something sold today), and his patents covered something that just about every commercial enterprise did. He may have had more patents than Edison, but unlike Edison, he never actually made or perfected any of these inventions himself.

This kind of patent jokingly became known as a "submarine" patent because it stayed hidden under the surface for a long time and then arose and blasted you out of the water when you least expected it. That was because at the time, patent applications were kept secret in the U.S. until they were granted and Lemelson never filed his patents outside the U.S. where they would be published. By making the date of a patent based on its earliest effective filing date instead of its grant date, and by publishing pending patent applications, it essentially ended new submarine patents starting June 8, 1995.

And while the courts of justice grind slow, they grind fine. In *Symbol Technology v. Lemelson* (Fed. Cir. 2005), the Court of Appeals for the Federal Circuit, which handles all patent appeals from the Federal District Courts, ruled that Lemelson's patents were unenforceable because of the way he got them, namely by intentional delay or as the courts have been calling it "late claiming". This undoubtedly caused his successors to suffer some heartburn at their Aspen ski lodges, but presumably not Mr. Lemelson, as he is likely too busy filing further continuing applications in the heavenly Patent Office.

So to recap, in the U.S., a patent having a filing date on or after June 8, 1995 has a term of 20 years from its earliest effective filing date. Patents filed before June 8, 1995 have a term which is the longer of 20 years from its earliest effective filing date or 17 years from its date of issue. In the rest of the world, patents typically last 20 years from their filing dates. In Japan, patents are also granted for 20 years from their filing dates, but not longer than 15 years from their grant date.

Patent Term Extensions

As mentioned earlier, a pharmaceutical patent can have a longer term based on a *patent term extension*, which may be granted based on national laws which provide additional patent life to make up for some of the time lost on a patent during drug registration. Typical patent term extensions are for up to five years in the U.S. (called "Patent Term Restorations" in 35 USC 156) and other similar patent term extensions are available in major countries such as Europe, Australia and Japan. Canada is an exception and allows no additional patent term. Recall Canada strongly favors generics over innovative pharmaceuticals, so it is being consistent in not encouraging pharmaceutical research by refusing to provide extended terms for pharmaceutical patents.

Patent term extensions do not actually extend the patent term for all of the claims of a patent. Instead, the patent term is extended only for claims covering the approved drug product. Thus a patent term extension will not keep competitors from filing for similar drugs to the innovator's drug after the nominal term of a patent, but it will help protect the approved drug product from becoming a generic drug.

The FDA takes the position that any subsequently approved drug containing the same "active moiety" as the approved drug product is also entitled to the same patent term extension and indicates this in an online listing for all approved drug products called the Orange Book. ("Active moiety" refers to the portion of the drug molecule that is biologically active. Different salts, esters and hydrates of the same active drug contain the same active moiety.)

Patent term extensions in the U.S. are allowed only for patents that cover the first approval of a drug product and must be filed in the U.S. within 60 days of the date that the drug product was approved. If you miss that date by even one day, only a private Act of Congress can help. In addition only one patent may be extended for an approved drug product and remaining patent life including extension cannot exceed 14 years. Details for obtaining such extensions may be found in the statute—just Google "35 USC 156". There is one exception for veterinary drugs. A patent for a new veterinary drug product may be extended even if the same drug was previously approved for human use.

In two recent cases, *Photocure v. Kappos* and *Ortho-McNeil v. Lupin* (Fed. Cir. 2010), the Court expanded the scope of patent term extensions by confirming eligibility for patent term extensions for new patents covering new approved products consisting of isomers or esters of drug compounds which had been previously approved.

In Europe, there are similar rules for obtaining patent term extensions (called "Supplementary Protection Certificates"), but in addition, under recent European Court cases, one can obtain patent term extensions for patents covering a new use of an old drug or covering new combinations of old drugs. Those two important additional types of extensions are not available under U.S. law.

HOW ARE PATENTS OBTAINED

First to Invent vs. First to File

Patents are typically filed first in one's home country. In the U.S., the first to *invent* used to be entitled to the patent. Outside the U.S. the first to *file* is awarded the patent. Effective March 16, 2013 in accordance with the America Invents Act (AIA), the U.S. joined the rest of the world and now awards patents to the first to file.

Previously, if there was a dispute between inventors in the U.S., it was resolved in a proceeding called an "interference" in which each party tried to establish it invented first. Interferences occurred in very few cases and were fought in the U.S. Patent and Trademark Office (PTO) in a formal procedure which was expensive, time consuming and contentious. They also could be settled using a private arbitrator if both parties agreed to do so, often with the understanding that the winner, whoever it turned out to be, licensed the loser. Outside the U.S. there is no need for such a procedure since the first to file is entitled to the patent, unless the second to file can prove the first to file had stolen the invention from him. The new U.S. rule on first to file thus puts the emphasis on prompt filing in the U.S. While the one year so-called "grace period" still remains, it is now personal to the inventor and generally does not cover third party disclosures of the invention made prior to the date of filing.

One of the urban legends about patents is that the way for an inventor to prove his date of invention is to mail to himself a sealed envelope containing his invention disclosure to get a postmark establishing his date of invention. Some inventors tend to be secretive and even a little paranoid (in a good way) so they like this idea. The only problem is that such a procedure cannot legally establish a date of invention. This is because the patent laws provide that a date of invention can only be established if a third party, who is not an inventor, corroborates the date of the invention in writing.

Today one does not even have to establish a date of invention as the first to file is awarded the patent regardless who invented first. But if you want to establish a date of invention, prepare a written disclosure of it and have a non-inventor read it and sign and date it. That establishes the legally required corroboration.

Provisional Applications

The current trend in filing patents in the U.S. is to first file a *provisional* application because the governmental filing fees are low and it is not necessary to provide claims or other formalities. To perfect the provisional application, you must file a complete application within a year of the filing date of the provisional and you get the benefit of the earlier filing date of the provisional. You can file anything as a provisional application, such as a scientific paper, and use it as the basis of a patent application within the year provided. The only catch is that the provisional must provide the proper legal disclosure for a patentable invention in order to get the benefit of its filing date when you file the complete application later.

If you don't file the complete patent application within the year, the provisional dies in secret and has no further use. A bonus for filing the provisional application is that it does not count towards the life of the patent, so you really get 21 years from the filing date of a provisional patent application if you perfect it with a regular patent application filing within one year.

Foreign Filings

Currently the U.S. Patent Office publishes only complete applications within about 18 months of filing. Foreign patent applications are typically filed in foreign countries within 12 months of the date of the first non-provisional or regular filing. This is based on an international treaty (Paris Convention) that most countries belong to which provides that the first filing date of a patent becomes its effective filing date in all other countries, so long as it is filed in those other countries within one year of its first filing anywhere.

In order to file outside the U.S., you must first obtain a license to do so from the U.S. Patent Office. Licenses are automatically granted by the U.S. Patent Office after filing a patent application, unless your patent happens to relate to national security, atomic bombs, and the like. In the unlikely event you do not get the automatic license, it would not be wise to file abroad until you've seen your patent lawyer, since your U.S. patent could be invalidated and you will likely have violated data security laws. If you do file abroad by mistake without a license, you can request a retroactive license if the subject matter is not of the kind to raise an issue and without having the FBI call for a chat.

(19) Europäisches Patentamt
European Patent Office
Office européen des brevets

(11)   **EP 1 010 431 B1**

(12)   **EUROPEAN PATENT SPECIFICATION**

(45) Date of publication and mention
of the grant of the patent:
30.03.2005 Bulletin 2005/13

(51) Int Cl.⁷: **A61K 38/16**, A61P 1/04,
A61P 43/00, A61K 38/48,
A61P 21/02

(21) Application number: 99203735.8

(22) Date of filing: 16.12.1994

(54) **Botulinum toxins A or B for treating pain associated with smooth muscle spasms**

Botulinustoxine A oder B zur Behandlung von Schmerzen verbunden mit Glattmuskelkrämpfen

Toxines botuliniques A ou B pour le traitement de la douleur liée à des spasmes des muscles lisses

(84) Designated Contracting States:
DE ES FR GB IT

(30) Priority: 28.12.1993 US 173996

(43) Date of publication of application:
21.06.2000 Bulletin 2000/25

(60) Divisional application:
04000166.1 / 1 421 948

(62) Document number(s) of the earlier application(s) in
accordance with Art. 76 EPC:
95906674.7 / 0 737 074

(73) Proprietor: **Allergan, Inc.**
Irvine, CA 92612 (US)

(72) Inventors:
• **Aoki, Roger K.**
Laguna Hills, CA 92653 (US)
• **Grayston, Michael W.**
Irvine, CA 92714 (US)
• **Carlson, Steven R.**
Laguna Niguel, CA 92677 (US)

• Leon, Judith M.
Laguna Niguel, CA 92677 (US)

(74) Representative: HOFFMANN - EITLE
Patent- und Rechtsanwälte
Arabellastrasse 4
81925 München (DE)

(56) References cited:
WO-A-94/28923   WO-A-95/05842
WO-A-95/28171

• JANKOVIC J ET AL: "THERAPEUTIC USES OF
BOTULINUM TOXIN" NEW ENGLAND JOURNAL
OF MEDICINE, THE,US,MASSACHUSETTS
MEDICAL SOCIETY, WALTHAM, MA, vol. 324,
no. 17, 25 April 1991 (1991-04-25), pages
1186-1194, XP000550926 ISSN: 0028-4793
• ANDERSON T.J. ET AL: 'Botulinum toxin
treatment of spasmodic torticollis' JOURNAL OF
THE ROYAL SOCIETY OF MEDICINE vol. 85, no.
9, September 1992, LONDON, GB, pages 524 -
529

EP 1 010 431 B1

3. First page of a European Patent

(12) INTERNATIONAL APPLICATION PUBLISHED UNDER THE PATENT COOPERATION TREATY (PCT)

(19) **World Intellectual Property Organization**
International Bureau

(43) **International Publication Date**
12 October 2006 (12.10.2006)

PCT

(10) **International Publication Number**
WO 2006/107921 A2

(51) **International Patent Classification:** Not classified

(21) **International Application Number:**
PCT/US2006/012426

(22) **International Filing Date:** 4 April 2006 (04.04.2006)

(25) **Filing Language:** English

(26) **Publication Language:** English

(30) **Priority Data:**
60/668,942   5 April 2005 (05.04.2005)   US

(71) **Applicant** *(for all designated States except US)*: **ALLERGAN, INC.** [US/US]; 2525 Dupont Drive, Irvine, California 92612 (US).

(72) **Inventors; and**

(75) **Inventors/Applicants** *(for US only)*: **FERNANDEZ-SALAS, Ester** [ES/US]; 1710 Rocky Road, Fullerton, California 92831 (US). **STEWARD, Lance, E.** [US/US]; 9 Woodfern, Irvine, California 92614 (US). **AOKI, Kei, Roger** [US/US]; 2 Ginger Lily Court, Coto De Caza, California 92679 (US).

(74) **Agents: STATHAKIS, Dean, G.** et al.; c/o ALLERGAN, INC., 2525 Dupont Drive, Irvine, California 92612 (US).

(81) **Designated States** *(unless otherwise indicated, for every kind of national protection available)*: AE, AG, AL, AM, AT, AU, AZ, BA, BB, BG, BR, BW, BY, BZ, CA, CH, CN, CO, CR, CU, CZ, DE, DK, DM, DZ, EC, EE, EG, ES, FI, GB, GD, GE, GH, GM, HR, HU, ID, IL, IN, IS, JP, KE, KG, KM, KN, KP, KR, KZ, LC, LK, LR, LS, LT, LU, LV, LY, MA, MD, MG, MK, MN, MW, MX, MZ, NA, NG, NI, NO, NZ, OM, PG, PH, PL, PT, RO, RU, SC, SD, SE, SG, SK, SL, SM, SY, TJ, TM, TN, TR, TT, TZ, UA, UG, US, UZ, VC, VN, YU, ZA, ZM, ZW.

(84) **Designated States** *(unless otherwise indicated, for every kind of regional protection available)*: ARIPO (BW, GH, GM, KE, LS, MW, MZ, NA, SD, SL, SZ, TZ, UG, ZM, ZW), Eurasian (AM, AZ, BY, KG, KZ, MD, RU, TJ, TM), European (AT, BE, BG, CH, CY, CZ, DE, DK, EE, ES, FI, FR, GB, GR, HU, IE, IS, IT, LT, LU, LV, MC, NL, PL, PT, RO, SE, SI, SK, TR), OAPI (BF, BJ, CF, CG, CI, CM, GA, GN, GQ, GW, ML, MR, NE, SN, TD, TG).

[Continued on next page]

(54) Title: LIPOPHILIC DYE-BASED FRET ASSAYS FOR CLOSTRIDIAL TOXIN ACTIVITY

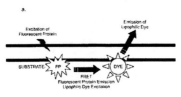

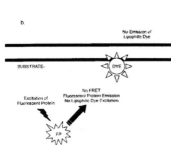

(57) **Abstract:** Compositions useful for detecting Clostridial toxin activity comprising a cell that comprises a membrane-associated Clostridial toxin substrate comprising a first member of a fluorescence resonance energy transfer pair; and a Clostridial toxin recognition sequence including a cleavage site; and a membrane-associated second member of the FRET pair; and methods useful for determining Clostridial toxin activity using such Clostridial toxin substrates.

WO 2006/107921 A2

4. Front page of a PCT Application

Patent Cooperation Treaty

There is also another treaty, the Patent Cooperation Treaty or "PCT", which allows a single place holder application to be filed within one year of the original filing date of a patent application, which reserves the right to file in most countries in the world without having to actually file a patent application in each country until 31 months after the original filing date or 19 months after the PCT filing. This gives the inventor or his company more time to evaluate the invention without loss of any rights before having to file it worldwide at significant expense. It also may provide enough time so that the patentability of the invention becomes clearer during prosecution of the patent in the home country patent office, though times for examination have been increasing and it is not unusual for a U.S. patent application to remain pending for 1–3 years before it is examined.

The rules are very unforgiving. If the 12-month foreign filing date is missed by even one day, the right to the earlier filing date is lost forever. If it is lost and if there was an intervening publication, even your own publication, disclosing your invention between your U.S. filing date and your foreign filing date, your foreign patent will not be valid.

The PCT application is relatively inexpensive to file as foreign patent costs go (about $4,000) and it reserves your rights in most major countries worldwide. Remember that within about six months after filing the PCT it is published for all to see. If you want to keep your invention a secret until it is patented, don't file it abroad and don't file a PCT.

Costs of Filing

Filing, obtaining and maintaining patents is not cheap. In addition to lawyer fees for preparation and prosecution before the

Patent Office, there are governmental filing fees, examination fees, grant fees and periodic maintenance fees over the life of a patent. Current costs for obtaining a U.S. pharmaceutical patent including legal fees and government charges average about $25,000: $7,500 to $15,000 for preparation and filing, the same for prosecution and grant, plus maintenance fees due at the 4th, 8th and 12th year anniversaries of the patent totalling another $13,000.

In most foreign countries the costs are generally higher due to translation costs and higher government application and issue fees and annual maintenance fees over the life of the patent. In the U.S., "Small Entities" (individual inventors or companies with less than 500 employees and Universities), and "Micro Entities" (individuals with a certain gross income limit who have filed fewer than 4 patent applications or persons associated with an institute of higher education) also get a break on U.S. Patent Office fees, and are generally charged 50% and 25% respectively of the fees charged to "Large Entities". The catch is that if and when a small or micro entity becomes a large entity e.g., by licensing the patent to a large entity, normal fees are due from that time forward. This can be a trap for the unwary as fee mistakes can invalidate a patent.

An agreement between member states of the European Patent Organization (EPO) called the London Agreement went into effect May 1, 2008 for patents granted in Europe on or after that date. That Agreement provides that you only have to translate the *claims* of an EPO filed patent into the language of the European country in which it is granted, rather than translate the whole patent document (except for Spain and Italy). This has brought about a significant reduction in the cost of obtaining patents in Europe by substantially reducing translation costs which typically accounted for as much as 80% of the cost of issuing a patent in non-English speaking countries in Europe.

In 2012, the European Council came to an agreement on the European Union's proposed "unitary patent system" which would provide a single patent filed in either French, German or English, covering all EU member states (except Spain and Italy who were pouting about their language being left out) and a single European patent court with branches located in Paris, London and Munich, having exclusive jurisdiction of infringement and revocation proceedings. No translations would be required. Following ratification by at least 13 member states including France, Germany and the UK, the unitary patent system is expected to come into force in 2015.

Currently one has to sue infringers in each EU country under each national patent with the potential for different results in different countries under differing national laws, not to mention the time, expense and uncertainty of multiple litigations. When implemented, this new system should greatly simplify obtaining, enforcing and defending patent rights in Europe.

PATENT CONTENTS

A patent consists of a multi-page printed document which gives the basic information about itself on the cover page which discloses the title of the patent, the name(s) and city address of the inventor(s) and the owner or assignee of the patent, along with other useful information. In the U.S., the inventor is the owner unless the patent is assigned to another. If the patent has been assigned and that assignment has been recorded in the Patent Office, the patent will also set forth the name and city address of the assignee. The cover page also gives a summary of the invention, but it is written when the patent is filed and it is rarely changed, so it is a summary of the application when filed rather than a summary of the patent when granted, and therefore it may not accurately describe the invention claimed.

Specification

The specification or body of the patent describes the invention and how it is to be used. It typically starts with a description of the field of the invention and describes what was known in the field before the invention was made, the so-called "prior art". It then describes the invention generally and then again in detail and offers examples of how it works. If it is a patent on a new chemical entity (NCE), it will describe exactly how to make it and what the chemical and physical characteristics of the new compounds are. If it is about a new medical use, it will describe dosage forms, suitable formulations and concentrations of drug to be used and the disease or condition to be treated.

Claims

At the end of the patent document are numbered paragraphs known as "claims". Claims are the heart and soul of a patent and define the rights granted to the patent holder as a deed to a piece of real property defines the property lines ("metes and bounds") of the property for the property owner. Litigation concerning a patent always focuses on the claims and each and every word in them. Skilled patent litigators often refer to infringers as *trespassers on the property* of the patent owner. So to understand a patent, you must first understand the claims.

The claims of a patent define the scope of the invention. Much time and attention is given to claims and that is what 95% of patent prosecution is about. When you submit the patent application, an Examiner reads it and must make a decision on whether to allow the claims you have presented to become part of a granted patent. Claims tend to be long-winded because the regulations require each claim to consist of a single sentence.

The broadest patents have the shortest claims. That is because the more you say about something, the more specific you become, which *narrows* the claim. The broadest claim is one that requires the least said about it. With claims, as with certain other matters in the field of human endeavor, the less said the better.

For example the shortest and therefore broadest claim I am aware of is in U.S. Patent No. 3,156,523 for an element, Americium, discovered by Glenn T. Seaborg and colleagues at the University of California at Berkeley (a little plug here for my *alma mater*). Claim 1 reads "Element 95". You might think an *element* could not be patented, but recall the transuranium elements are not naturally occurring, so element 95 is man-made and thus patentable. Now that is a broad claim. Seaborg also discovered elements 94–102 and 106 including plutonium (94) and was awarded the Nobel Prize for Chemistry in 1951. His name will live on forever as he also got possibly the longest lasting award one can think of: element 106 was officially named Seaborgium in 1994.

The goal of a typical patent attorney is to cover the invention with as broad a claim as possible, usually claim 1. After claim 1, a number of more detailed claims typically follow, i.e., narrower claims until the last claim that is generally the narrowest. There is no law requiring this order, so occasionally a broader claim may come later in the series.

For pharmaceutical formulations covering commercial drug products, it is a good idea to have some narrow claims in your patent which cover the commercial drug formulation more or less exactly. While such narrow claims would be relatively easy to design around, it can be the best way to protect a commercial drug against a generic copier who simply copies the commercial formula.

There are generally two types of claims. One is called independent and the other is called dependent. The independent claim stands on its own, while the dependent one refers to another claim. The dependent claim is a shorthand way of claiming a new feature of the invention without reciting all the

United States Patent Office

3,156,523
Patented Nov. 10, 1964

1

3,156,523
ELEMENT 95 AND METHOD OF PRODUCING
SAID ELEMENT
Glenn T. Seaborg, Chicago, Ill., assignor to the United
States of America as represented by the United States
Atomic Energy Commission
No Drawing.   Filed Aug. 23, 1946, Ser. No. 692,730
12 Claims.   (Cl. 23—14.5)

The present invention relates to a new transuranic element. More particularly it is concerned with the transuranic element having atomic number 95, now known as americium having the symbol Am, isotopes thereof, compositions containing the same, and methods of producing and purifying said element and compositions thereof.

The expression "element 95" is used throughout this description to designate the element having atomic number 95. Reference herein to this element is to be understood as denoting the element generically whether singly or in combination, unless otherwise indicated by the context.

As far as is presently known two isotopes of americium have been synthesized in identifiable quantities, i.e., $_{95}Am^{241}$ and $_{95}Am^{242}$. The former isotope is an alpha emitter having a half-life of 500 years, while the latter is a short-lived (17–18 hours half-life) beta emitter which is transformed relatively rapidly into element 96^{242}, known as curium and having the symbol Cm, an isotope of another new transuranic element and an alpha emitter having a half-life of about five months. The alpha particles emitted from this isotope have a range in air of 4.75 cm. A second isotope, $_{96}Cm^{240}$, is produced by the bombardment of 94^{239} with alpha particles. This isotope has a half-life of thirty days and is also an alpha emitter. The alpha particles produced thereby have a range of 5.0 cm. in air.

In accordance with the present invention, it has been found that these isotopes of element 95 can be produced in a variety of ways such as, for example, by bombarding plutonium produced in a neutronic reactor, which consists essentially of isotope 94^{239} together with a relatively small concentration of isotope 94^{240}, with subatomic particles, e.g., deuterons or neutrons. In preparing element 95 by the bombardment of plutonium with deuterons, for example, these subatomic particles should generally have energies of the order of at least 10 mev. and preferably energies of 14 to 16 mev. or higher. The synthesis of element 95 in this manner is thought to involve at least a portion and very probably all of the nuclear reactions indicated below:

$$94^{239} + {_1}d^2 \longrightarrow 95^{241} + {_0}n^1$$
$$94^{239} + {_1}d^2 \longrightarrow 95^{240} + 2{_0}n^1$$
$$95^{240} + {_1}d^2 \longrightarrow 94^{241} + {_1}p^1$$
$$94^{241} \xrightarrow[\text{40 years}]{B^-} 95^{241}$$
$$94^{241} + {_1}d^2 \longrightarrow 95^{241}$$
$$94^{239} + {_1}d^2 \longrightarrow 95^{240}$$

In general, it has been found that element 95 is most conveniently synthesized in a neutronic reactor operated at a relatively high power level (about 200 kw.) for an extended period of time (approximately 100 days). A suitable neutronic reactor which may be employed in the preparation of element 95 is described and claimed in co-pending application for United States Letters Patent, Serial No. 568,904 of Enrico Fermi and Leo Szilard, filed December 19, 1944, now Patent No. 2,708,656. In such reactors a fissionable isotope, such as U^{235} in natural uranium, undergoes fission and releases fast neutrons in excess of the neutrons absorbed in the fission process.

2

The fast neutrons are slowed down to approximately thermal energies by impacts with a moderator such as graphite or deuterium oxide, and the resulting slow neutrons (energies of 0–0.3 electron volt) are then absorbed by U^{235} to produce further fission and by U^{238} to produce U^{239} which decays through 93^{239} to 94^{239}. This self-sustaining chain reaction releases tremendous amounts of energy, primarily in the form of kinetic energy of the fission fragments. With such reactors the maximum reaction rate for steady state operation is determined by the maximum rate at which the heat of reaction can be removed. The rate of production of plutonium in such reactors may thus be equated, approximately, to the power output of the reactor, and amounts to about 0.9 gram of 94^{239} per megawatt day when operating with decay of 93^{239} to 94^{239}.

A portion of the 94^{239} thus produced in the reactor under such conditions absorbs neutrons to form the isotope 94^{240}. In neutronic reactors operated under the general conditions of power level and time indicated above the absorption cross-section of 94^{239} for the formation of 94^{240} is rather large, amounting for thermal neutrons to nearly one-half the cross-section for the fission of 94^{239}. Thus plutonium produced in the above manner frequently contains as much as 2% of the isotope 94^{240}. The latter isotope is an alpha emitter and also undergoes spontaneous fission to a slight extent (half-life for the process is 10^{11} years). If this isotope is maintained in a neutronic reactor for a substantial period after its formation, it is transformed into the next heavier isotope which, in general, constitutes about .01 percent of the total plutonium produced under conditions of power level and time indicated above. As previously pointed out, 94^{241} is a beta emitter and decays into 95^{241}.

In a natural uranium pile, or neutronic reactor operating at such substantial powers and for substantial periods of time, the formation of element 95 (isotopes 95^{241} and 95^{242} and 96^{242}) is presumed to be synthesized in accordance with the following series of nuclear reactions:

$$Pu^{239} \xrightarrow{B^-} 95^{241} \longrightarrow 96^{242}$$

etc. (nuclear reaction scheme)

The mechanism of formation of 94^{241} as indicated by the nuclear reactions written above is such that its concentration in pile uranium is proportional to the third power of the specific neutron exposure and the ratio of its concentration to that of 94^{239} is proportional to the second power of the specific neutron exposure. Hence, the amount of 95^{241} which is formed per day per unit of plutonium in the free or combined state is proportional to the second power of the specific neutron exposure of the uranium from which the plutonium was formed. Inasmuch as the decay of 94^{241} to 95^{241} occurs during as well as after the neutron bombardment period, the percentage of the latter in the transuranic fraction can be controlled by varying

3,156,523

11

This procedure was repeated, precipitating from an even smaller volume (0.75 μl.) with very little, if any, plutonium peroxide being formed. The amount of plutonium remaining with element 95 appeared to be very insignificant. A count of the entire sample was made in a vacuum low geometry chamber. The total count of element 95 was found to be 1.13×10^2 c./m.

It is to be understood that the specific compounds described above and the foregoing examples are merely illustrative of the present invention and are in no way to be construed as limitative thereof. It will be apparent to those skilled in the art that the general procedure set out in the above description is susceptible of numerous modifications without departing from the spirit of the present invention. For example, it should be noted that while element 95 can be removed from solutions of neutron irradiated uranium or plutonium by means of the carrier methods herein set forth, said element may also be removed from other aqueous or non-aqueous liquid media in addition to those resulting from the solution of uranium or plutonium in a suitable acid utilizing methods similar in principle to those herein set forth.

What is claimed is:

1. Element 95.

2. The isotope of element 95 having the mass number 241.

3. The isotope of element 95 having the mass number 242.

4. A method of separating element 95 values from an aqueous solution thereof which comprises contacting the solution with a substantially insoluble compound having an anion which forms a substantially insoluble lanthanide rare earth compound whereby the element 95 values become associated with said compound, and separating said compound and associated element 95 values from said solution.

5. A method of separating element 95 values from an aqueous solution thereof which comprises contacting the solution with a soluble compound capable of ionizing to

12

produce an anion which forms an insoluble lanthanide rare earth compound whereby an insoluble precipitate of element 95 and said anion is formed, and separating said precipitate from the solution.

6. A process for the removal of element 95 values from a solution containing said values, which comprises contacting said solution with a lanthanide rare earth fluoride precipitate carrier for said element and separating said carrier precipitate and associated element 95 values from the solution.

7. The process of claim 6 in which the carrier is lanthanum fluoride.

8. The process of claim 6 in which the carrier is cerous fluoride.

9. A salt of americium and a mineral acid.

10. Americium dioxide.

11. Americium trichloride.

12. Americium hydroxide.

References Cited in the file of this patent

UNITED STATES PATENTS

2,577,097	Werner	_____	Dec. 4, 1951
2,708,565	Fermi et al.	_____	May 17, 1955

OTHER REFERENCES

Grosse: Journal of the American Chemical Society, vol. 57, pages 440 and 441 (1935).

Hahn et al.: Chemical Abstracts, vol. 30, page 8007, 1936.

McMillan et al.: Physical Review, vol. 57, pp. 1185 and 1186, 1940.

Smyth: A General Account of the Development of Methods of Using Atomic Energy for Military Purposes Under the Auspices of the U.S. Government, pp. 94–99 (1945). Superintendent of Documents, Washington, 25, D.C.

Seaborg: Chemical and Eng. News, vol. 25 (1947), pp. 358–360.

6. Last page with claims of U.S. Patent No. 3,156,523

old features again. For example claim 1 below is an independent claim followed by claim 2, a dependent claim:

1. A method for treating spasticity comprising administering to a spastic patient an effective amount of a botulinum toxin.

2. The method of claim 1 wherein the botulinum toxin is botulinum toxin type A.

There are other forms of claims with names and much more could be said about them, but the take home on claims is that *claims define the scope of the invention* and that is what a patent covers, no more and no less. When someone asks what does the patent cover, you must *read the claims* to find out.

WHAT IS NOT PATENTABLE?

Laws of Nature

Abstract ideas, physical phenomena and laws of nature are not patentable, as well as mathematical expressions and purely mental steps such as algorithms and computer programs, except when patented in combination with hardware. Recently, the courts have allowed so-called "business method" patents, such as the one-click ordering of merchandise on the internet, which previously were denied as being purely mental steps. Cloning methods are patentable, but not cloned human beings, though genetically engineered bacteria and mice, among other living things, have been patented.

The famous Harvard "onco-mouse", altered to develop cancer, was the first patented transgenic mammal, patented in the U.S. in 1988 under U.S. Patent No. 4,736,866, but it still bothers some people that "life" can be patented. In 2004, the European Patent Office finally upheld the corresponding European patent, which initially had been approved in 1992, against objections by church, environmental and animal protection groups, including Greenpeace, who had argued for cancellation on the grounds that it violated the dignity of living beings.

The U.S. Supreme Court weighed in on the issue of what is patentable in 2010 in the case of *Bilski v. Kappos* by ruling a method of hedging risk in the energy market was not patentable as an attempt to patent an abstract idea. The Court further ruled that the Federal Circuit Court's previous rulings on the subject, which required a "machine or transformation" test as the sole test to determine when a process was patentable subject matter, was not the only test.

In the medical treatment field, the Supreme Court also unanimously decided the important *Mayo v. Prometheus* case (Supreme Court 2012). The Prometheus invention related to a method of optimizing therapeutic efficacy for treatment of a medical disorder by identifying relationships between concentrations of certain metabolites in the blood and the likelihood that a dosage of a certain drug (thiopurine) would prove either ineffective or cause harm. Claim 1 for example stated that if blood levels of a certain metabolite exceeded a certain level after a specified dose of that drug, then such dose would produce toxic side effects.

The Court found that the claimed relationship was a consequence of the way in which thiopurine compounds are metabolized by the body, which is an entirely natural process. And so a patent that simply describes that relation sets forth a natural law and is therefore not patentable. The conclusion here is that a newly discovered law of nature is not patentable and the application of that newly discovered law is also not patentable if the application merely relies upon known elements.

Natural Substances

What about newly discovered naturally occurring compounds in plants, frog skins, ocean sponges or the human body itself? Until recently, the answer was that an otherwise novel, naturally occurring compound was patentable if the discovery was in identifying and separating it in practical quantities if that had not been done before. I previously called that the "compound-in-a-bottle" test. If a naturally occurring compound or protein in the body did not previously exist in practical quantities in a bottle, you could probably patent it in the U.S.

However, in 2013, the U.S. Supreme Court finally took up the question of whether isolated natural human genes were "new", as required by the patent laws (35 USC 101). As background, a company called Myriad had discovered the precise location and sequence of two naturally occurring genes (BRCA1 and BRCA2). Myriad used these newly discovered natural genes to devise an expensive cancer diagnostic test to detect mutations in those genes which are responsible for many hereditary breast and ovarian cancers.

The District Court held that Myriad's gene claims were invalid because they covered products of nature and were therefore not "new" and therefore not patentable. The Federal Circuit reversed and held both isolated DNA and synthetic DNA were "new" and therefore patent eligible because the act of isolation created a new product sufficiently different, both structurally and functionally, from that which existed in the natural genome, so that the isolated DNA was no longer a natural product. This decision was expected in light of similar rulings in Europe and Australia and the fact that the U.S. Patent Office had granted thousands of such patents in the past.

But in *Association for Molecular Pathology v. Myriad Genetics* (Supreme Court 2013), the Supreme Court again reversed and held in a unanimous decision that a naturally occurring DNA segment is a product of nature and therefore not new and therefore not patent eligible merely because it has been isolated and while Myriad discovered the location of the BRCA genes, that discovery, by itself, does not render those genes "new" and therefore patent eligible.

However, the Court also ruled that synthetic or complimentary DNA (so-called "cDNA" which is DNA with non-coding segments removed) is patent eligible because it is made in a laboratory and is not naturally occurring. Complementary DNA is commercially valuable because it is generally used to genetically engineer cells. The Court also carefully noted this case did not address the patentability of method claims or the patentability of DNA in which the order of the naturally occurring nucleotides has been altered.

This Supreme Court ruling will likely have significant effects on the patentability of other "naturally occurring" chemicals, such as hormones, antibodies and other biological molecules first discovered and isolated from humans, plants or animals. Note that isolated natural DNA, as well as naturally occurring compounds isolated from nature, remain patentable in Europe and

Australia and elsewhere outside the U.S. under their respective national laws.

Inherency

Also not patentable are inventions that are inherent e.g., the discovery of the actual mechanism of action of a drug for treatment of a given cancer, when it was previously known to use the drug to treat the same cancer. The mechanism of action was inherent in the previous use of the drug and is therefore not separately patentable, even though it was never known before. However, knowledge of such a mechanism could be used to discover a new compound to treat the same disease or a new use for the same cancer drug (e.g., for a new type of cancer or another disease) and that would not be inherent and so could be patentable. In short, discovering *why* something works may be good science, but it may not be patentable. A good example of this concerns the world's first synthetic drug.

Story of Aspirin

The glycoside salicin, the bitter principle in willow leaves and bark, had been used for thousands of years as a folk remedy for treatment of pain, inflammation and fever. In the body, salicin is metabolized into salicylic acid, which was effective, but was hard on the stomach. This much was known on August 10, 1897 when Felix Hoffmann, a chemist at a German dyestuffs company called Bayer, added an acetyl chemical group to the salicylic acid molecule and came up with acetyl salicylic acid or aspirin. Arguably, this was the beginning of the modern drug era. Hoffmann got a patent for aspirin too, U.S. Patent No. 644,077 granted in 1900.

In more recent times, my friend the late Sir John Vane, the British pharmacologist, was awarded the Nobel Prize in Medicine in 1982 and a British Knighthood for discovering the

UNITED STATES PATENT OFFICE.

FELIX HOFFMANN, OF ELBERFELD, GERMANY, ASSIGNOR TO THE FARBEN-
FABRIKEN OF ELBERFELD COMPANY, OF NEW YORK.

ACETYL SALICYLIC ACID.

SPECIFICATION forming part of Letters Patent No. 644,077, dated February 27, 1900.

Application filed August 1, 1898. Serial No. 687,385. (Specimens.)

To all whom it may concern:

Be it known that I, FELIX HOFFMANN, doctor of philosophy, chemist, (assignor to the FARBENFABRIKEN OF ELBERFELD COMPANY, of New York,) residing at Elberfeld, Germany, have invented a new and useful Improvement in the Manufacture or Production of Acetyl Salicylic Acid; and I hereby declare the following to be a clear and exact description of my invention.

In the *Annalen der Chemie und Pharmacie*, Vol. 150, pages 11 and 12, Kraut has described that he obtained by the action of acetyl chlorid on salicylic acid a body which he thought to be acetyl salicylic acid. I have now found that on heating salicylic acid with acetic anhydride a body is obtained the properties of which are perfectly different from those of the body described by Kraut. According to my researches the body obtained by means of my new process is undoubtedly the real acetyl salicylic acid

$$C_6H_4\left\langle {}^{OCO.CH_3}_{COOH}. \right.$$

Therefore the compound described by Kraut cannot be the real acetyl salicylic acid, but is another compound. In the following I point out specifically the principal differences between my new compound and the body described by Kraut.

If the Kraut product is boiled even for a long while with water, (according to Kraut's statement,) acetic acid is not produced, while my new body when boiled with water is readily split up, acetic and salicylic acid being produced. The watery solution of the Kraut body shows the same behavior on the addition of a small quantity of ferric chlorid as a watery solution of salicylic acid when mixed with a small quantity of ferric chlorid—that is to say, it assumes a violet color. On the contrary, a watery solution of my new body when mixed with ferric chlorid does not assume a violet color. If a melted test portion of the Kraut body is allowed to cool, it begins to solidify (according to Kraut's statement) at from 118° to 118.5° centigrade, while a melted test portion of my product solidifies at about 70° centigrade. The melting-points of the two compounds cannot be compared, be-

cause Kraut does not give the melting-point of his compound. It follows from these details that the two compounds are absolutely different.

In producing my new compound I can proceed as follows, (without limiting myself to the particulars given:) A mixture prepared from fifty parts of salicylic acid and seventy-five parts of acetic anhydride is heated for about two hours at about 150° centigrade in a vessel provided with a reflux condenser. Thus a clear liquid is obtained, from which on cooling a crystalline mass is separated, which is the acetyl salicylic acid. It is freed from the acetic anhydride by pressing and then recrystallized from dry chloroform. The acid is thus obtained in the shape of glittering white needles melting at about 135° centigrade, which are easily soluble in benzene, alcohol, glacial acetic acid, and chloroform, but difficultly soluble in cold water. It has the formula

$$C_6H_4\left\langle {}^{OCOCH_3}_{COOH} \right.$$

and exhibits therapeutical properties.

Having now described my invention and in what manner the same is to be performed, what I claim as new, and desire to secure by Letters Patent, is—

As a new article of manufacture the acetyl salicylic acid having the formula:

$$C_6H_4\left\langle {}^{O.COCH_3}_{COOH} \right.$$

being when crystallized from dry chloroform in the shape of white glittering needles, easily soluble in benzene, alcohol and glacial acetic acid, difficultly soluble in cold water, being split by hot water into acetic acid and salicylic acid, melting at about 135° centigrade, substantially as hereinbefore described.

In testimony whereof I have signed my name in the presence of two subscribing witnesses.

FELIX HOFFMANN.

Witnesses:
R. E. JAHN,
OTTO KÖNIG.

7. Patent for Aspirin

precise mechanism of action of *why* aspirin worked, through inhibition of certain enzymes that produced inflammatory compounds called prostaglandins. While the discovery was brilliant, it would not have been patentable as being inherent. A discovery or invention may also not be patentable because it doesn't meet the basic requirements for patentability.

BASIC REQUIREMENTS FOR PATENTABILITY

The rules are deceptively simple. Apart from the requirements for a proper written disclosure of the invention (a written description and an enabling disclosure), an invention must be:

- new
- useful
- novel
- non-obvious
- invented by the applicant for the patent

New

The requirement for "new" relates to what is considered patentable subject matter, which was discussed immediately above.

Useful

Just about any alleged use for an invention is sufficient to meet the legal obligation for an invention being useful, though it must have a "substantial utility" and provide a specific benefit in currently available form (*Brenner v. Manson* (Supreme Court 1966)). A pharmaceutical patent will typically allege a number of possible medical uses for the invention and the patent is valid even if only a single use is ultimately found to be practical. In biotech, portions of genes involving simple sequences of amino acids known as "expressed sequence tags" (ESTs) useful only for research have been rejected as not having met the legal requirement for being useful (*In re Fisher* (Fed. Cir. 2005)).

Some promising drug candidates have the opposite problem; too many uses or as I call it, "a drug in search of a disease". While they seem to have great potential for use as a drug for a variety of medical indications, they rarely become commercially useful for the reason that they are too non-specific and have too many side effects. As a colleague of mine once said, it is hard to come up with a melody when you play all the keys of the piano at the same time. However, the usefulness required by the patent laws does not mean commercially useful or even FDA approvable, so that is not an issue for patenting such a compound.

Novel

For U.S. patents filed before March 16, 2013, the requirement for "novelty" means that no one patented or published the exact same invention anywhere in the world or used it or sold it or offered it for sale in the U.S. or had public knowledge of it more than a year before the invention was made.

For U.S. patent applications filed on or after March 16, 2013, the one year grace period only applies to disclosures by the inventor or by others who derived their information from the inventor and foreign use and sale are also bars to patentability.

Outside the U.S., there is generally no so-called "grace period" of one year, though there are limited exceptions. Therefore public disclosure of an invention by anyone including the inventor before filing for patent will generally act to invalidate the patent outside the U.S. Private disclosure without a secrecy agreement or non-disclosure agreement could also have the same result.

The publication date of an article is considered to be the date it became available to the public and not the date it was submitted for publication. Any public presentation, for example, at a scientific meeting, that discloses an invention acts as a bar to a patent on that invention outside of the U.S. if the patent has not been filed before the disclosure. However, the one year grace period could allow the patent to be obtained in the U.S. if a patent application was filed within a year of the disclosure (by the inventor on applications filed on or after March 16, 2013).

Experimental Use Exception

An exception to this general rule is if the invention was being tested before completion (the so-called "experimental use" exception), but that can be difficult to establish legally and could result in loss of patent rights if it is determined the invention was already perfected. In general, the courts look to see if the alleged experimental use was (1) accessible to the public and/or (2) commercially exploited.

In the pharma field, clinical trials have been held not to be an experimental use where the inventors did not know if their formulations would work for their intended purpose until after the clinical trial (*In re Omiprazole Patent Litigation* (Fed. Cir. 2008)). More recently, in *Dey v. Sunovion* (Fed. Cir. 2013), the Federal Circuit likewise held a clinical trial was not a public use due to confidentiality with the clinical trial administrator and the fact the subjects were given incomplete descriptions of the treatment formulations. However, in *Pronova v. Teva* (Fed. Cir. 2013), the Federal Circuit held a patent invalid as a public use where a shipment of the drug product that was claimed in the subject patent was sent to a skilled outside researcher for testing to confirm its content without any restrictions, and the product's formulation was disclosed in detail to the researcher, and that the confirmatory testing was performed by the researcher.

Does the America Invents Act affect the foregoing? Effective March 16, 2013, clinical trials conducted outside the U.S. which do not meet the experimental use exception could be used to invalidate the patent if the clinical trial was found to be "available to the public". As a result, the safest thing for an inventor to do is to file at least a provisional application in the U.S. before making any public disclosures of the invention to avoid possible loss of rights.

Non-obvious

This is almost always the main question concerning patentability. Typically, an invention is new, useful and novel or no one would bother filing a patent on it. The law says non-obviousness must be viewed from the perspective of one of ordinary skill in the subject matter to which the invention pertains, with knowledge of all prior public uses and publications relating to such subject matter, taken as a whole. The law of non-obviousness fills whole libraries so thankfully this book is not intended to go into it in any detail. However, that is what patent attorneys spend most of their time and your money on: trying to convince patent examiners that the invention in front of them is not obvious, or in front of judges and juries trying to convince them that it is.

In order to be rejected in the U.S. Patent Office on the grounds of non-obviousness (known in the trade as a "103 rejection" after the U.S. code section which defines non-obviousness), an Examiner may combine any number of prior publications that relate to your invention and reject your claims as being obvious in light of the combination. This is in contrast to a rejection for lack of novelty that requires that the disclosure of the invention in the prior publication be contained within a single document.

For example if you were claiming the first metal tennis racquet, the Examiner could reject you by combining one reference showing a conventional wooden racquet with a second reference showing that it was known to replace wood with metal in other sports equipment, such as skis. That would establish what the Patent Office would call a "prima facie" case of obviousness or obvious on its face. In order to overcome this rejection, the inventor would have to submit further argument as to why it would not be obvious to substitute metal for wood in a tennis racquet or that by doing so, one obtained certain unexpected results such as superior accuracy or faster ball speed off the racquet or whatever.

A finding of unexpected results typically overcomes the prima facie case of obviousness. That is why patent lawyers are always looking for *unexpected results* as it is often the key to obtaining a patent. (A friend of mine, a pilot, once told me that actors were always looking for inspiration and pilots were always looking for a place to land. I asked what about lawyers? He said lawyers were always looking for a situation in which a great deal of money was about to change hands!)

The Supreme Court has recently handed down its first new decision on obviousness in 40 years. The new case, *KSR v. Teleflex* (Supreme Court 2007) concerned the validity of a patent covering a variable-height gas pedal. In holding the patent invalid, the Supreme Court made clear that *"the combination of familiar elements according to known methods is likely to be obvious when it does no more than yield predictable results"*. In other words, if common sense tells you something is obvious, and there are no unexpected results, then it is probably not patentable.

The *KSR* case overturned an important line of cases which the Court of Appeals for the Federal Circuit (CAFC or Federal Ciruit) had long advocated as the standard for determining obviousness (the so-called "teaching-suggestion-motivation" ("TSM") test. The TSM test requires that there be evidence of some teaching or suggestion or other motivation to combine prior art references to show obviousness, since otherwise any invention could be considered obvious by hindsight if all you had to do was find the parts of the invention in separate documents and simply say it would have been obvious to combine them to make the invention.

The *KSR* case concerned the patentability of a variable-height gas pedal that substituted an electronic means for controlling speed for a conventional mechanical cable. In restating the law of obviousness, the Supreme Court did not say that the TSM test was necessarily always a bad test, (though Mr. Justice Scalia said in oral argument that he thought the test was "gobbledygook"), the Court concluded it was too rigid a test and it was certainly not the only test that should be applied, and although there had to be *some reason* articulated to combine references, that reason might even be just plain old common sense.

In fact the Supreme Court suggested in *KSR* that one of the reasons for combining references could even be "obvious to try". If such a standard were to be routinely applied in chemical cases, few chemical patents would be found valid. An "obvious to try" standard essentially substitutes hindsight for a more intellectually rigorous analysis to determine whether an invention would have been obvious to an ordinarily skilled artisan at the time the invention was made, a bit like Monday-morning quarterbacking. Since *KSR*, the Federal Circuit and the lower courts have been working out the modified standard for obviousness.

The effect on pharmaceutical cases so far has been a tightening up of the standards for patentability, though evidence of "unexpected results" or a finding of synergy (where a combination of drugs results in more than what would be expected from their additive effects) often carries the day for patentability, though not always.

For example, in a recent case decided by the Federal Circuit after *KSR*, a patent covering a certain stereoisomer (stereoisomers are molecules that are identical chemically, but have different physical confirmations in space, like left- and right-handed gloves, that can behave differently in biological systems and are typically present together in the parent compound as a mixture of stereoisomers) that had little or no unexpected advantages over the previously known parent compound from which it was separated. As a result, the Court found that the patent covering that separated stereoisomer, the well-known ACE inhibitor Altace (ramipril) used for treating high blood pressure, was invalid for obviousness over its previously known parent compound (*Aventis v. Lupin* (Fed. Cir. 2007)).

On the other hand, in a case decided 6 days earlier involving another stereoisomer pharmaceutical product Lexapro (escitalopram), the same court held the patent valid on the grounds that the patent owner was able to show unexpected benefits of Lexapro over the previously known parent compound from which it was separated and there was evidence that Lexapro was not capable of being separated from the known parent compound using methods known to an ordinarily skilled artisan (*Forest Labs v. Ivax* (Fed. Cir. 2007)).

However in a third case *Pfizer v. Apotex* (Fed. Cir. 2007), Pfizer's patent for the discovery of a particularly advantageous salt of a drug was held invalid as being obvious on the grounds there were 53 FDA approved salts and Pfizer admittedly tested each one to identify the best one for its drug. The fact that there were a finite number of choices made the choice obvious despite the unexpected results.

Finally, in *Novo v. Caraco* (Fed. Cir. 2013), the Court affirmed the District court finding that the discovery by Novo of the synergistic effects of combining two conventional type II diabetes treatments was predictable, thereby rendering the combination obvious. In short, even the discovery of a novel, synergistic combination of two old diabetes drugs was nonetheless held obvious to try when such results were predictable from the prior art.

So one can conclude from these cases that decisions on obviousness will continue to be fact specific, though it is likely that

KSR will affect patentability for the more simple pharmaceutical and biological products and it will affect patentability for medical devices in that it is generally more difficult to show unexpected results with mechanical inventions than with chemical and biological inventions.

These same basic concepts also apply outside the U.S. to patents, although different language may be used. For example, in Europe, the European Patent Office and the courts talk of the requirement for "inventive step", but it is the same basic concept as the requirement for "non-obviousness".

INVENTORSHIP

U.S. law provides that a patent may only be granted to the inventor(s) of the invention as defined by the claims. An inventor is one who first conceived the invention, where conception is defined as the formation in the mind of the inventor of a definite and permanent idea of the complete and operative invention. Someone who was involved in the invention may not be an inventor if that person played no part in conceiving the invention. This is different from authorship on a scientific paper where anyone who contributed to the paper can be an author.

Inventors for a patent are only those persons who *conceived* the invention, which includes reducing it to practice if the reduction to practice included an inventive contribution to one or more of the claims. Thus one who conceives of using a drug for a new treatment might be a co-inventor with a doctor who discovered the necessary dosage forms or dose of the drug or treatment regimen to obtain the desired result. If the amounts and dosage form and treatment regimen used was conventional, then the doctor would not likely be a co-inventor, but merely one who assisted the inventor.

The reason that the correct inventors must be named on a patent is that having the wrong inventors may invalidate the patent, though if an innocent mistake is made without deceptive intent, inventorship can be corrected at any time. Outside the U.S., the issue of inventorship is not as important, as patents may be filed in the name of the assignee company for example. U.S. patent attorneys must therefore identify the true and correct inventors for each patent application and not have too many or too few. Also, who is the first or last listed name on a scientific paper is important to scientists, but has no meaning in a patent.

A curious aspect of U.S. patent law is that each inventor named in a patent is a joint owner of the whole of the patent and therefore each inventor can license the patent to a third party without notice or payment to the other inventors. So if someone agrees to give you an exclusive license to his patent, make sure he is the sole inventor or has an assignment from the other inventors or else one of the other inventors could legally license the same patent exclusively to someone else. However, all inventors must agree to litigate the patent since their rights to the patent may be affected by litigation.

INEQUITABLE CONDUCT

A patent may be granted if it meets the forgoing requirements, but may be held unenforcible by a court if it is determined the patent was obtained through inequitable conduct due to "unclean hands" during the prosecution of the patent before the U.S. Patent Office. In *Therasense v. Becton Dickinson* (Fed. Cir. 2011) (en banc), the Federal Circuit rewrote the law of inequitable conduct. In the patent in suit, the lower court had held the patent unenforcible due to inequitable conduct because the patent attorney did not disclose to the U.S. Patent Office during a protracted 13 year prosecution an inconsistent statement made in the prosecution of the corresponding European patent.

In reversing the lower court, the Federal Circuit recognized the problems created by the expansion and overuse of the inequitable conduct doctrine. While the unclean hands doctrine remains for egregious acts of deliberate fraud, it is no longer applicable unless it is proven by clear and convincing evidence that the patentee acted with specific intent to deceive.

PROOF OF INVENTION

Another urban legend about patents is that you have to be able to prove that your invention works before you can file a patent. While that sounds reasonable, it is not true. There is no requirement that you must have proof that your invention works before you file your patent application. You can hypothesize a plausible invention and file a patent application on it. That is because the law provides that the filing of a patent application is the legal equivalent to having completed the invention. (The legal way to say this is the filing of a patent application is a *constructive reduction to practice*.)

You can also think up any number of pharmaceutical new use inventions and file patents on them. For example, if I conclude that floor wax can treat cancer based only on my belief that it can, I can file a patent application on that new use for floor wax with no data or proof of any kind that it treats cancer. This is a valid patent application and *if* a patent were granted on it, it would be a valid patent so long as the patent described in reasonable detail how to make and use the invention. But that does not really answer the question of whether such a patent in fact *would be* granted by a patent examiner.

If a patent examiner does not believe your invention is credible, he can ask for proof before granting it. If you have no proof, you will typically not obtain your patent. So, you say, you do need proof before you can get a patent. Well, the answer is sometimes you do and sometimes you don't, but it is still the case that you don't need proof *before you file* the patent application. Many worthwhile medical inventions are filed as patent applications long before there is any real clinical evidence that they work, though such proof may be forth-coming at a later time. And if the invention is explained in a credible way, proof may not be requested and the patent can properly be granted without proof. That is the beauty of the concept of "constructive reduction to practice".

Historically the practice of requiring proof to patent a drug actually started around the late 1800s and early 1900s when hucksters started patenting drug formulations and calling them *Patent Medicines*. These were mostly snake oil and other questionable nostrums for treating whatever ailed you and the Patent Office was being criticized for facilitating these scams by awarding patents. That was when the Patent Office started asking for proof of efficacy and denying patents for unproven remedies.

AMERICA INVENTS ACT

On September 16, 2011, the Leahy-Smith America Invents Act (AIA) was enacted into law. As mentioned earlier, the major change is a shift from first-to-invent to first-to-file for all U.S. patent applications filed on or after March 16, 2013. The following is a summary of the key changes:

- Conversion of the U.S. patent system from a first-to-invent priority to a first-to-file standard.

- The traditional one year grace period during which the inventor's own disclosures and those of third parties may not be used as prior art if they occurred within 12 months of the effective filing date of the invention has been modified to include only disclosures by the inventor himself or by third parties who derived their disclosure from the inventor.

• Foreign public use and sale are now considered prior art whereas previously only domestic prior public use and sale could invalidate a patent. Note the one year grace period also applies to such use or sales by the inventor.

• The law now provides a new defense to infringement based on prior commercial use called a "prior user defense" that would apply if the prior commercial use was maintained as a trade secret and therefore not invalidating prior art.

• Post Grant Review proceedings which allow third party challenges of a patent's validity in the Patent Office within nine months of grant. The Post Grant Review is somewhat parallel to post-grant oppositions in Europe and applies only to first-to-file U.S. patents (those filed on or after March 16, 2013).

• Patent owners now have the option to request a supplemental examination of a patent to correct mistakes or to eliminate potential defences, starting September 16, 2012.

• Failure to disclose the "best mode" in a patent application has been eliminated as an invalidity defense.

If the European experience is followed, probably the most important change in the AIA is the provision for post grant review. In Europe, many patents are subject to opposition by competitors after grant and these proceedings are costly and time consuming and take years to complete. In addition the U.S. legal standard for post grant review has a lower standard (preponderance of the evidence) in contrast to the higher court standard for holding a patent invalid (clear and convincing evidence).

The main difference with Europe however is that there is an estoppel associated with the U.S. post grant review in subsequent litigation asserting invalidity on any ground that reasonably could have been raised during the post grant review. That estoppel may discourage some competitors from requesting the new post grant review, since the patent would be significantly strengthened if it was upheld in the post-grant review by making it more difficult to invalidate at a later date in court.

Patent Exhaustion

The doctrine of patent exhaustion limits a patent owner's right to control what others can do with a patented item. Under the doctrine, the initial authorized sale of a patented item terminates all patent rights to that item. That is, the sale confers on the purchaser or any subsequent owner the right to use or sell the patented item as he sees fit. While the doctrine restricts a patent owner's rights as to the particular item sold, it leaves untouched the patent owner's ability to prevent the buyer from making new copies of the patented item.

In *Bowman v. Monsanto* (Supreme Court 2013), the issue was whether the doctrine of patent exhaustion permitted a farmer to reproduce patented soybean seeds through planting and harvesting of the purchased seeds without the patent holder's permission. The decision would have an enormous impact on many businesses besides agriculture, including gene therapies, vaccines, cell lines and even software, where patented inventions can be easily replicated or are even self-replicating, as with the patented seeds. In concluding there was no patent exhaustion in the case of self-replicating seeds, the Court explained that

> "… *by planting and harvesting Monsanto's patented seeds, Bowman made additional copies of Monsanto's patented invention and his conduct therefore falls outside the protections of patent exhaustion. Were it otherwise, Monsanto's patent would provide scant benefit…*"

since farmers would need to buy patented seed only once as they could then simply reproduce them through planting and harvesting.

TAKE HOME MESSAGE

- A patent is primarily a sword, not a shield; it has few defensive characteristics and gives you no affirmative right to use your patent, other than the right for a limited time to exclude others from making, using or selling your invention.

- A U.S. patent generally expires 20 years from the date of its earliest effective filing date, or the longer of that date or 17 years from its issue date if filed in the U.S. before June 8, 1995. A foreign patent expires 20 years from its filing date in that country.

- The life of one patent covering an approved pharmaceutical product containing a new drug may be extended by up to five years in the U.S., Europe and Japan to make up for some of the time lost in obtaining approval for marketing.

- Patents are typically filed in one's home country first and then abroad within 12 months to maintain the benefit of the initial filing date.

- Use of the PCT can reserve your foreign rights for an additional 19 months.

- To understand a patent, you must first understand the claims. Claims define the scope of an invention, as a deed defines property.

- To be patentable, an invention must be new, useful, novel, non-obvious and invented by the applicant.

- You do not need proof your invention works before you file a patent.

- An isolated naturally occurring DNA segment is not patentable in the U.S. as being a product of nature, though a synthetic gene is patentable.

- The America Invents Act changed the U.S. "first to invent" rule to the international "first to file" standard and added a post grant review opportunity for third parties within 9 months of grant of any patent filed on or after March 16, 2013.

The next Chapter discusses **Patent Enforcement and Infringement.**

Chapter 2

Patent Enforcement and Infringement

PATENT ENFORCEMENT

While the government grants a patent, it is up to the owner or exclusive licensee to enforce it in a court of law. The courts that have primary jurisdiction over patents in the U.S. are the Federal District Courts. These courts determine both validity and infringement of a patent at the same time. All appeals from a decision of one of the Federal District Courts are to a single appeals court, the Court of Appeals for the Federal Circuit in Washington, DC. The only appeal from that Court is to the U.S. Supreme Court. This results in a certain consistency in the Federal District Courts, though as they say, your mileage may vary.

Patent infringement determinations are also made by the U.S. International Trade Commission (ITC) where the infringement is alleged to result from importation of infringing goods into the U.S. under 19 U.S.C. 1337. The ITC has the authority to determine if the imported goods infringe a U.S. patent and if it finds the patent to be valid and infringed, it can issue an exclusion order to U.S. Customs to impound or seize the infringing goods to prevent their importation into the U.S., subject to final approval by the US Trade Representative. The ITC decisions are reviewable by the Court of Appeals for the Federal Circuit, the same court that hears patent appeals from all the U.S. Federal District Courts. A patent owner can bring actions before both the federal courts and the ITC.

Patent owners like the ITC because it is fast and will get a competitor off the market very quickly if successful. In the medical field, it is primarily used by device manufacturers, though there have been some drug cases brought before the ITC. In generic cases, a brand owner might consider an action in the ITC to stop the importation of the active drug if it is manufactured outside the U.S. and imported by the U.S. generic company for use in manufacturing the finished goods or if the infringing drug product itself is manufactured outside the U.S.

Outside the U.S., the court systems also vary and in some countries such as Japan and Germany, the civil courts decide infringement, but another specialized Patent Court or the Patent Office decides validity in a separate proceeding. As a result, one can sue an infringer and win a court case on infringement, but then the infringer can ask to have another court block the first court by holding the patent invalid. In the U.S. and U.K., the same court decides both validity and infringement at the same time, so there is more finality. The Courts that decide validity in effect second guess the Patent Office and decide whether the patent should have been granted in the first place. In the U.S. and most other countries, a patent is presumed valid, which means the infringer has the burden of persuading the Court that the Patent Office was wrong in granting the patent.

BURDEN OF PROOF

The burden of proof in a U.S. patent validity case is greater than the typical burden of proof in a civil case which requires "a preponderance of the evidence", i.e., 51%, but much less than the well-known criminal standard of guilt "beyond a reasonable doubt". The validity standard is in between the other standards and requires "clear and convincing evidence" of invalidity to overturn a patent. This is an important distinction as it means an infringer must provide persuasive evidence of invalidity to a judge or jury in order to overturn a patent. In short, close calls go to the patent owner.

The U.S. Supreme court agreed to hear an appeal in *Microsoft v. i4i Limited Partnership* (Supreme Court 2011) to consider whether the presumption of validity always requires "clear and convincing" evidence or in some instances may only require "a preponderance of the evidence" to invalidate a patent. The Court ruled that the tougher "clear and convincing" standard is appropriate in all cases, even when new reasons for invalidity are asserted which were not considered by the Patent Office when the patent was granted, which is what Microsoft alleged in its appeal.

TRIALS IN THE U.S.

U.S. patent cases are typically tried before a jury, though they may be tried before a judge only. For example, cases involving generic challenges to branded drugs are generally tried before a judge. On the whole, juries seem to like patents and tend not to overturn them on grounds of lacking validity as they don't feel comfortable in revoking a patent that has been granted by the United States Patent Office. Patent infringement cases can be very expensive and legal fees often cost each side in the millions of dollars.

TRIALS OUTSIDE THE U.S.

Judges decide patent infringement cases outside the U.S. With the exception of the U.K., costs in European countries tend to be significantly less than in the U.S., though the combined costs of multiple infringement cases going on at the same time in several European countries add up. This is due to the fact that while one can file a single patent application with the European Patent Office (EPO) to cover most European countries, the patent that results becomes a separate national patent in each country and each country retains jurisdiction over it in its courts for questions of infringement and validity. This allows the same patent to be held infringed in one European country by a given product and held not to be infringed by the same product in another and this has happened.

There have been numerous attempts to provide a true European-wide patent that could be enforced in a single European court, but up until recently the individual countries have not been willing to give up their sovereignty on this issue and the specific issue of which language(s) would be controlling has also prevented implementation. However, as mentioned earlier, Europe approved plans for a Unitary Patent System in 2012, with implementation expected by 2015, which will provide for a single patent to cover Europe, with only Spain and Italy opting out.

Things tend to work pretty slowly outside the U.S. especially in the third world. For example, Pfizer filed its patent for Viagra in China in 1994 and it was granted in 2001 and on the same day 13 Chinese pharmaceutical manufacturers requested it to be invalidated (while they were selling generic versions of Viagra). In 2004, the Chinese Patent Re-examination Board (PRB) held the patent invalid based on insufficient disclosure, but that decision was overturned on appeal in 2006 and affirmed in 2007 by the Beijing People's High Court, leaving Pfizer with only 7 years left on its patent until it expires in 2014. Unfortunately for Pfizer, the case was remanded to the PRB for further examination on the opponent's other grounds for invalidity which were not addressed in the original PRB decision. By the time the Chinese courts are finished with the patent, it will likely be expired. This type of treatment for patents is not uncommon in many parts of the third world such as India, China and even South America, where lip service to pharmaceutical patents is traditional.

Branded drug makers are finding authorities in emerging markets are more concerned with maintaining low prices for drugs than fostering intellectual property. With governments often paying for drugs, the tendency for those governments is to hold patents for expensive drugs invalid to open the way to domestically produced inexpensive generic drugs. Recent examples of this include Gilead's popular HIV and hepatitis B drug Viread (tenofovir), which was held invalid in Brazil in 2008 and invalid by China's State Intellectual Property Office in 2013 and GSK's patent on its cancer drug Tykerb and Novartis' patent on its cancer drug Glivec, held invalid in India.

Another way emerging countries such as China and India deal with expensive patented drugs is through compulsory licensing under laws that allow for compulsory licensing of a drug if it is not made available to the public at a reasonable price. For example, in 2012, India issued a compulsory license to Bayer's cancer drug Nexavar (sorefinib) saying its $5,600/month price was not a "reasonable price". Under the license, a local generic manufacturer will have to pay Bayer a 6% royalty and will sell the same drug for $175/month.

With this level of price disparity, one can hardly blame emerging countries for taking such actions when dealing with expensive life-saving new drugs for its poor. Innovative drug companies have started providing discounts in such countries, but they will need to think of new and better ways to deliver new drugs to emerging countries at affordable prices to avoid compulsory licensing and having their patents held invalid due to high prices.

INFRINGEMENT

In order to infringe a patent, a product or process must incorporate each and every feature or element of at least one of the claims of a patent. For example, if a patent claim covers four features or elements of a product, in order to infringe, the product would have to include each and every one of those four features or elements. It could have additional features or elements and still infringe, but it will not infringe if it does not contain all four.

Patents can be infringed either literally or by equivalents. Literal infringement means that the product or process incorporates each and every element of a single claim. For example, if I have a patent that claims a certain device consisting of five elements attached to a wall with a nail, you are a literal infringer if you manufacture, use or sell the same device containing at least the same five elements attached to a wall by a nail. But what happens if you have the same device, but it is attached to the wall with a screw? That is not *literal* infringement, but it might be infringement under the *doctrine of equivalents*.

The federal courts developed the doctrine of infringement by equivalents to avoid the situation in which an insignificant or insubstantial change to a product or process would allow an infringer to get around an otherwise legitimate patent. In this case, the patent owner should have claimed a wall fastener and not a nail to insure literal infringement, but a court could decide that in the context of the invention, a screw was the *equivalent* of a nail and find the device infringed under the doctrine of equivalents.

Of course nothing is simple and many a dusty tome is devoted to what is and what is not an equivalent. Unfortunately, while this doctrine is well intended, it creates what I like to modestly call (with apologies to Werner Heisenberg) the *Voet Patent Uncertainty Principle*. That is, you would like to know if your gizmo infringes a certain patent. You ask a patent attorney and he will do a search at some expense to you and will tell you it does not infringe any patents *literally* because you do not have one of the specifically claimed elements in your gizmo. However, he goes on to say, it might infringe under the doctrine of equivalents because your gizmo performs substantially the same function in substantially the same way to obtain substantially the same result as the patented invention (like substituting the screw for the nail when it is used as a wall fastener). That is not much comfort and is often frustrating to patent owners because of the lack of certainty. But sometimes that is just the way the patent cookie crumbles, so patent owners have to live with the uncertainty until a court rules on the matter or the case is settled. However, in the meantime, you can get an opinion.

INFRINGEMENT AND VALIDITY OPINIONS GENERALLY

It is often the case that a company obtains an infringement or validity opinion on a patent if it is interested in enforcing it or if it is worried that the patent might be enforced against it. These opinions are performed by an in-house patent attorney or more generally by an outside patent attorney or firm. There is a second reason a possible infringer might obtain such an opinion and that is for legal protection against a claim of willful infringement.

In a successful infringement case, a court can award additional damages up to three times actual damages if the court finds the infringer "willfully" infringed. A normal defense to such a claim of willfulness is having previously obtained an opinion from an independent, competent counsel that the patent was invalid or not infringed and that the opinion was relied upon. In this way, the opinion shields the infringer from the claim that he acted willfully as he can claim he relied on the opinion. This is the so-called "advice-of-counsel" defense.

The need for such an opinion to avoid a finding of willfulness has now been altered by a recent case, *In re Seagate Technology* (Fed. Cir. 2007). In a rare unanimous decision overruling prior precedent and establishing a new standard of determining willful patent infringement, the Court held that willful infringement enhanced damages now requires a showing of "objective recklessness". The decision abolishes the long-standing "duty of care" standard previously required.

This will make it more difficult for patent holders to prove willfulness and thereby obtain additional damages. In the same decision, the Court also held that the accused infringer's reliance on the "advice-of-counsel" defense did not require waiver of the attorney-client privilege. However, it may be difficult to explain to a jury why someone should not be considered a willful infringer if he knew about the patent and/or was accused of infringement and simply ignored the patent. A better defense is to obtain a properly drafted opinion that the accused product is not infringing or that the patent is invalid, or both, and rely on it.

This is also the point at which counsel is asked if the patent in question is "*good* and *strong*". This is a hard question to answer because the person asking the question assumes if the patent is good and strong they will win. In fact, these adjectives taken literally are somewhat contradictory. "Good" means the patent broadly claims the subject matter and thereby provides good protection against infringers. "Strong" means the patent is defensible in court and that usually requires the claims to be narrow in scope so as to be defensible against attacks on validity, since a broad patent is generally more easily attacked on grounds of invalidity than a narrow patent. Nonetheless counsel knows that the real question behind the question asked is "*will we win the case?*" and he answers accordingly.

If counsel cautions against litigation because of some possible problems with enforcing a patent, he often hears something like "well then why did we get the blasted patent in the first place if we can't sue on it!" The answer is that patents have a variety of uses, only one of which is marching into court. These include strategic uses such as licensing, getting access to new products through cross-licensing, simply being an asset of a company that is important to the overall value of the enterprise, and in a rare defensive aspect, provide for future defense by keeping on hand some patents that cover competitors' products, so that when a competitor claims you have infringed one of his patents, you can claim right back and that often leads to a settlement at little or no cost.

I have seen this happen many times, since having some skin in the game is usually necessary for a favorable settlement. In addition, multiple patents relating to your own products and potential improvements have a cumulative effect and act to discourage investment by competitors in areas close to those you have patented. Finally, jurors tend to be a little confused by patents and trial lawyers like to say that their client has his own patent on his product, so he should not be held liable as an infringer of another's patent. This as we know makes no sense whatsoever as a patent is a sword and not a shield and having a patent cannot legally shield you from a claim of infringement, but that argument continues to be made successfully to jurors every day.

Regarding patent strategies, one of the best is to try to patent your competitors' products. This seems odd since it would seem you should be patenting your own products. But this strategy flows naturally from the nature of a patent right that is only to exclude others. For example, you might be the first to discover acrylic polymers have advantages over other classes of polymers for making intraocular lenses to replace cloudy natural eye lenses or cataracts. Your competitor in that field may be secretly work-ing on his own new lens with his own acrylic polymer different from the polymer in your new lens, but if his polymer falls within the scope of your broad patent covering the use of any acrylic polymer for making intraocular lenses, you have, in effect, pat-ented his future product even though you did not know what it was.

In short, the best patent defense can be patent offense and this technique allows one to convert the offensive nature of a patent into a defensive one. So when a competitor comes threatening with a patent covering one of your important products, you reply confidently that you have a patent covering one of his really important products and he can pound sand.

INFRINGEMENT OPINIONS

In the case of an infringement opinion, the attorney compares the potentially infringing product or process with the claims of the patent to determine if the claims cover the product or process. In order to do this, the attorney must read the patent and review the file history of the patent to determine the scope of the claims, i.e., what the claims cover and what they do not cover literally and by the aforementioned doctrine of equivalents. That is because the file history of the patent includes the patent prosecution before the Patent Office that typically consists of written rejections by patent examiners and written replies by patent attorneys giving reasons why the examiner incorrectly rejected the claims presented for examination.

Statements made by inventors or their attorneys during patent prosecution in the U.S. Patent Office are taken into consideration in defining the breadth or meaning of the claims. So if during prosecution of the patent, an attorney makes a statement as to what a patent claim is intended to cover and what it does not cover, the patent owner cannot later say in an infringement case that his claim covers something his attorney gave up earlier during prosecution to obtain the patent. (This is called *prosecution history estoppel*.)

Patent attorneys therefore have to be very careful about what they write to the Patent Office and that leads to the practice of asking for personal interviews with the Examiner rather than putting forth arguments in writing. After the interview, the Examiner or attorney may write a few lines about what was said for the record, but that usually does not result in any significant problems for the patent owner.

Interestingly most of the rest of the world's courts don't seem to care very much if at all about what was said in obtaining the patent in their country's patent offices and the judges decide what a patent covers, i.e., the scope of the claims, independently of what the patent prosecutors said to obtain it.

VALIDITY OPINIONS

In order to prepare a validity opinion, a patent attorney will review the file history of the patent in the U.S. and corresponding applications abroad. He will review the so-called "prior art" references (prior patents or publications related to the invention) cited by the various patent offices and the inventor and will likely conduct an independent search for additional prior art references to see if there are any disclosures of the invention or offers of sale before the patent application was filed which could invalidate it. The purpose is to try to find anything that would cast doubt on the validity of the patent. The possible infringer's attorney is looking for evidence that the patent is invalid, while the patent owner wants to avoid any surprises and evaluate the strength of his case.

DAMAGES AND INJUNCTIONS

If a court finds a party has infringed a valid and enforceable patent, the court awards damages for the infringement and generally issues a permanent injunction barring the infringer from making the product until the patent expires. In the U.S., damages take the form of either lost profits or a reasonable royalty. Attorney's fees are also awarded in exceptional cases such as willful infringement or bad faith litigation. Outside the U.S., the loser pays a substantial portion of the winner's attorney's fees in patent cases. Damages in the U.S. can be very large, sometimes hundreds of millions of dollars or more, though typically smaller awards are made. In Hatch Waxman cases involving challenges of branded drug patents by generics, only injunctions may be granted and no damages are awarded, though attorney's fees may be granted in an exceptional case to either winning side.

In a recent landmark decision, the U.S. Supreme Court ruled in *eBay v. MercExchange* (Supreme Court 2006) that permanent injunctions are no longer mandatory in a successful patent infringement case and that courts in patent cases must apply the same four-part test used for determining the imposition of injunctive relief that is used by the courts in other disputes:

- whether there is irreparable harm
- whether an adequate remedy otherwise exists
- whether the injunction would be in the public interest
- the balance of hardships between the parties

This is one of the most important new developments in patent law. It was brought on by the new reality that many products, especially in the telephonic, internet and computer areas, are now complex systems. To require that the entire system be enjoined, when the thing that infringed represents but a tiny part of the system, is not reasonable. In effect, this creates a de facto compulsory license if the infringer wants to keep using the patent.

For pharmaceutical infringement cases, and especially brand versus generic cases, it is doubtful that this case will lead to any significant change in the granting of injunctions, though it might in the situation of a patent for an important life-saving drug that the patent owner did not manufacture, as the four criteria would be on the side of the company to remain the supplier of the drug to the public. The "adequate remedy" would be money damages rather than an injunction.

FDA SAFE HARBOR

In another potentially far-reaching decision, the Supreme Court decided *Integra Lifesciences v. Merck* (Supreme Court 2005) concerning the meaning of the so-called "FDA exemption" for infringement under the patent statute (35 U.S.C. 271(e)(1)) which provides a "safe harbor" for acts which might otherwise infringe a patent if the infringing acts are "reasonably related" to development of information for submission to FDA. The Federal Circuit had construed the statute narrowly and held that preclinical research was not covered by the exemption.

The patents owned by Integra involved peptides that contained a certain sequence of amino acids within a peptide chain. The peptides modulate cell interactions and affect the development of blood vessels or angiogenesis. Integra filed a patent infringement action against Merck alleging that the use of the patented compounds in preclinical research by Merck constituted patent infringement.

The Supreme Court concluded that the statute should be interpreted broadly and that the safe harbor was not to be limited to infringing acts during clinical trials, but also included infringing acts undertaken during early research work on possible drug candidates, even if one or more of the candidates failed and information concerning them was never submitted to the FDA. The Supreme Court further indicated by footnote that the ruling was not necessarily intended to apply to patents in the biotech field known as "tool patents".

Tool patents are patents which involve patented methods for doing research that do not form a part of a finished drug product and are not used in its manufacture or use. In effect, the Supreme Court left the issue over the enforceability of such tool patents for another day. This is good news for many researchers in the biological field as a variety of reagents, enzymes, plasmids and other "research tools" are available commercially and to have to obtain a patent license for each and every one of them is simply not practical.

On remand to determine if the patents were enforceable under the Supreme Court's new interpretation of the statute, the Federal Circuit held in 2007 that the statute as now interpreted by the Supreme Court provided "safe harbor" for Merck's research activities and Integra could not successfully sue Merck for patent infringement.

A dissenting Judge opined that the decision effectively eliminated protection for research tool inventions since two of the patents in suit applied only to laboratory methods without the possibility of submission to the FDA and therefore the two patents were directed to research tools.

Two recent decisions on the scope of the FDA safe harbor came in *Classen v. Biogen* (Fed. Cir. 2011) and *Momenta v. Amphastar* (Fed. Cir. 2012). In the first case, Biogen was conducting post-approval studies on whether timing of vaccinations influenced risk of certain immune-mediated disorders. The studies were not mandated by FDA, though Biogen would normally have to submit the results of such a study to FDA. Classen sued Biogen claiming infringement of its patents on methods of immunization. The District Court ruled that Biogen's activities were protected by the FDA safe harbor. On appeal, the Federal Circuit ruled that the FDA safe harbor does not apply to information that "may be" routinely reported to FDA long after marketing approval was obtained.

In the *Momenta v. Amphastar* case, Momenta sued Amphastar on a patent covering an analytical method associated with manufacturing the approved drug, which testing was necessary to satisfy FDA requirements. A different Federal Circuit panel came to a different decision on somewhat similar facts and ruled the FDA safe harbor does apply to certain post-approval activities where the submissions to FDA were required to maintain FDA approval. The Court's decision in *Momenta* turned on the fact that the post-approval testing was required by FDA, while the tests in the *Classen* case were not required by FDA, even though once done, they were reportable to FDA.

TAKE HOME MESSAGE

• U.S. patents are enforced in the federal courts, generally in a jury trial, or by the International Trade Commission (ITC); brand versus generic cases are decided by a Federal District Court judge without a jury, or the ITC.

• A patent is presumed valid and an infringer has the burden of proof to overturn a patent based on clear and convincing evidence.

• Damages for infringement are either lost profits or a reasonable royalty.

• A product or process can infringe literally or under the doctrine of equivalents.

• To infringe a patent, the infringing product or process must incorporate each and every element of at least one claim in a patent.

• Under the *Seagate* case, it is no longer necessary to get a patent opinion to shield an accused infringer from a claim of willful infringement, though it still might be a good idea to have one.

• Under the *eBay* case, patent owners who win patent infringement actions no longer have the right to mandatory permanent injunctions.

- Under the *Merck-Integra* case and related cases, the FDA safe
harbor exemption from infringement applies to preclinical
research as well as clinical research and certain post approval
activities, so long as the research is reasonably related to
commercial drug development and the post-approval activities relate to information required by FDA.

The next chapter discusses **Pharmaceutical, Biological and
Medical Device Patents.**

Chapter 3

Pharmaceutical, Biological and Medical Device Patents

PHARMACEUTICAL PATENTS GENERALLY

Pharmaceutical patents are generally no different than other patents, except that under current U.S. law, a generic manufacturer can obtain the right to copy an innovative drug under certain circumstances if there is no valid patent covering it. This puts the onus on innovative drug manufacturers to protect their investment in the development and registration of their innovative drugs by obtaining and maintaining as many patents as they can that cover them. Typical pharmaceutical patents cover active drug compounds, their intermediates, metabolites, hydrates, salts and esters; combinations with other active drugs; methods of manufacturing the active drug and its intermediates; different methods of medical treatment using the drugs including novel indications and dosage regimens; formulations for the drug including new dosage forms; devices containing the drugs such as skin patches, drug delivery systems, etc.

HIERARCHY OF PATENTS

Compound Patents

The best pharmaceutical patent is a compound patent. This type of patent claims the active drug compound as well as its salts, esters and hydrates. It also typically covers a broad range of similar compounds to prevent a competitor from making a chemically similar drug. One common strategy is to file a broad patent on the compound, and then file a continuing application narrowly covering the active drug agent that is expected to become the approved product. This will result in the granting of two patents with the same expiration date, both covering the approved product. The first one will be "good" as it is broad and the second will be "strong" as it is narrow.

The reason the compound patent is the best pharmaceutical patent is that it covers a drug product no matter how it is formulated, no matter how it is made, no matter what it is sold for and no matter what use it is put to, as long as it contains the patented compound. According to a recent Court of Appeals decision which overturned a lower court ruling on this issue (*SmithKline v. Apotex* (Fed. Cir. 2004)), even the *amount* of that compound is not important, so that a drug product will infringe a compound patent even if it contains only a trace of the patented compound and even if an infringer did his best to try to keep that trace out of his product.

Medical Use Patents

The next most valuable type of pharmaceutical patent is a medical use patent. This type of patent covers the approved medical use or indication of an approved drug product. It can also cover unapproved medical uses. Typically, a medical use claim for treatment of a specific disease or condition is directly infringed only by a patient with that disease or condition or by the doctor for prescribing it, but not by the drug product manufacturer. However, the law makes one that actively induces another to infringe liable as a direct infringer. When a drug product is put on the market, it must contain instructions for use and these instructions provide the necessary "active inducement" to charge the manufacturer with infringement. As a result, a medical use patent will effectively prevent infringement of a drug product labelled for the patented use.

What about infringement of off-label patents, that is, patents which cover a medical use *not* on the label of a drug product, since many drugs today are used extensively by doctors for off-label medical uses? That is a more difficult question to answer and that is one reason why a compound patent is better than a use patent, since there is infringement with a compound patent regardless of the use or whether the use is approved or not.

There are two general situations in which off-label infringement occurs. The first is off-label use where an infringing product is labelled and sold for a given use, but prescribed by physicians for a patented use not on the FDA approved label. In order to show inducement of infringement, the patent owner would have to provide evidence that the drug manufacturer knew of the off-label use and actively induced others to infringe. This tends to be an issue that revolves around obtaining evidence of knowledge and intent of the drug manufacturer, including evidence of any overt acts to induce infringement.

Examples of activities that could suggest active inducement are any promotional or informational activities for the off-label use by the manufacturer or by third parties connected to the manufacturer in one way or another, such as statements by company sales people, company website references to the indication or educational programs for physicians to teach the off-label use that are directly or indirectly sponsored by the manufacturer.

The second off-label use is in the context of an abbreviated new drug application (ANDA) filing for a generic drug. Until 2003, it was common practice for innovators to list off-label patents in the FDA Orange Book which would then require generic companies to file Paragraph IV certifications which would allow the patent holder/innovator to file suit against the generic company for patent infringement and would prevent the FDA from approving the generic drug for 30 months. The current case law (_Warner-Lambert v. Apotex_ (Fed. Cir. 2003)) and related FDA regulations and federal legislation make it clear that innovators can no longer list off-label patents in the Orange Book. This is covered in more detail in Chapter 6.

One way a generic company can avoid a use patent properly listed in the Orange Book is by requesting labelling which omits the patented use by filing a so-called "Section 8" Statement (covered in more detail in Chapter 4). In a 2012 precedential decision, the Federal Circuit held for the first time in _AstraZeneca v. Apotex_ (Fed. Cir. 2012) that an ANDA applicant who files a section 8 statement for a product with a method of use patent and accordingly does not seek approval for that patented use, cannot be found liable for inducement of infringement of the patent during a Paragraph IV litigation.

The Federal Circuit was not convinced by AstraZeneca's practical argument that pharmacists and doctors can substitute a generic product for all indications once the generic product is approved, regardless of the labelled uses and concluded in a Paragraph IV setting, that a patented method of using a drug can only be infringed by filing an ANDA that seeks approval to market the drug for that use.

This is a significant change in the law and will encourage generic manufacturers to use the section 8 statement to insure avoidance of a brand's secondary method of use patents when the patents for the drug's compound and primary use have expired or been held invalid. Finally, the innovator may still be able to sue for infringement of that off-label use patent once the generic product is being sold on the market if there is evidence of actual inducement for the patented use.

Formulation Patents

The third basic type of patent for drug products is a formulation patent that typically covers the active drug agent in the specific formulation for use in the body. Sometimes, the formulation patent covers a unique excipient, such as a stabilizer or preservative used in the formulation. A formulation patent offers the least desirable patent protection because typically it can be avoided by using a different formulation. However, in the context of an ANDA submission for a generic drug, a formulation patent, no matter how narrow, may be ideally suited to prevent copying of the drug by a generic company.

That is because of the regulatory requirement for therapeutic equivalence that a generic drug must meet. While a generic drug is allowed to have minor differences in the formulation or even in the active drug agent, typically that would require clinical trials to establish therapeutic equivalence since the generic drug and the reference drug would not be "the same". To avoid the expense and time of clinical trials, most generic companies simply copy the innovator's drug formulation more or less exactly and try to invalidate the formulation patent.

Therefore even a very narrow formulation patent can be extremely valuable in preventing generic copying, even though it would be easy to get around the patent by reformulating. Patent holders should not forget to obtain very narrow formulation claims covering an innovator product in addition to broad ones, as narrow formulation claims are also easier to defend against attacks on validity.

BIOLOGICALS PATENTS

Patents for biologicals are no different in principle than patents for pharmaceuticals, except that they claim recombinant products, proteins, monoclonal antibodies, nucleic acids and synthetic DNA sequences and the like and their methods of manufacture and use. According to FDA, biological products, like other drugs, are used for the treatment, prevention or cure of disease in humans. However, in contrast to chemically synthesized small molecules, which have a well-defined structure and can be thoroughly characterized, biological products are large and complex in structure and often not fully characterized, as they are derived from living material—human, animal or microorganism.

Even though antibiotics are often produced by a biological process such as fermentation, they are handled by FDA administratively as drugs rather than biologics, as are hormones such as insulin and human growth hormone. On the other hand, all blood products, allergens, vaccines, products containing cells or microorganisms, most protein products and all recombinant products, are handled administratively as biologics regardless how they are made.

Since 2005 a number of generic biotechnology drugs have been approved in Australia, Europe and India as "biosimilars". In March 2010, President Obama signed into law healthcare reform legislation known as the "Patient Protection and Affordable Care Act" which contains provisions establishing for the first time an abbreviated regulatory pathway for generic versions of biological medicines in the U.S. This important new law is discussed in detail in Chapter 7.

MEDICAL DEVICE PATENTS

Typical medical device patents cover stents, intraocular lenses, heart-lung machines, etc. and they follow the same basic principles for patents in general. The big difference between patents for medical devices and patents for pharmaceuticals is that only the latter may be listed in the FDA Orange Book and come within the scope of the Hatch Waxman Act. As a result, under current U.S. law, medical devices may not be genericized as pharmaceuticals. However, there are regulatory procedures for medical devices that allow them to be commercialized based on similarity to an approved medical device and that is discussed in more detail in the next chapter.

TAKE HOME MESSAGE

- There are three basic types of pharmaceutical patents: compound, method of use and formulation.

- Compound patents provide the best protection for a drug product because they broadly cover a compound no matter how made or used.

- Method of use patents typically provide intermediate protection, especially for approved medical use claims.

- Formulation patents generally provide the least protection, but still provide good protection against a generic company that copies the patented formulation.

- Medical devices and biologics do not fall under the scope of the Hatch Waxman Act for FDA approval of generics.

The previous three chapters have discussed patents, the first leg of the three-legged stool of product life-cycle management. The next two chapters discuss the second regulatory leg: **U.S. Food and Drug Administration** and related **Drug Product Exclusivity**.

Chapter 4

Overview of FDA

FDA GENERALLY

The U.S. Food and Drug Administration (FDA) is a governmental agency charged with insuring that the nation's food
supply is unadulterated and medicines and medical devices are
safe and effective. Generally speaking, in order to market a new
or generic drug or Class III medical device or biological in the
U.S., one must first obtain pre-market approval from the FDA.
Over-the-counter (OTC) non-prescription medicines such as,
for example, headache and cough/cold medicines are regulated
by monograph, which means the FDA establishes written guidelines for these products, and if you meet the guidelines, you can
sell the product without pre-market approval.

Products containing herbs and other natural ingredients that
do not make medical use label claims generally do not require
pre-market approval under current law. If the FDA has evidence
that they are unsafe, the FDA can remove them from the market. The most recent case in point is ephedrine-containing
OTC products. This is in contrast to drugs and medical devices
that must prove their safety and efficacy before marketing is
permitted.

Other countries have similar agencies regulating drugs sold in that country. Approval by one major country does not provide approval in another, though some of the smaller countries will accept a drug for sale in its country if it is approved by a major country's health agency under what was called a Certificate of Free Sale, now called a Certificate of Pharmaceutical Product. In addition, there are regional approval systems such as the European Medicines Agency (EMA) in Europe where approval by that agency allows marketing in the countries of the European Union (EU).

However, generally, one must satisfy each major country's FDA equivalent Ministry of Health in order to market a drug product in that country. This requirement to duplicate clinical studies in many major countries to obtain pre-market approval for the same drug product adds significantly to the time and cost of development of innovative drugs and slows down the delivery of potentially life-saving medicines to the public.

ORIGINS OF FDA

The modern FDA began in 1906 with the passage of the Federal Food and Drug Act. Prior to that time, the states had primary control over food and drugs. The 1906 Act was the result of a national furor over improper conditions in the meatpacking industry that Upton Sinclair wrote about in *The Jungle*. This began a pattern for the next century where new laws regulating food and drugs were enacted in response to terrible conditions or accidents. The 1906 law had no pre-market approval aspects and drugs were required to be in accordance with the standards of strength, quality and purity set out in the *United States Pharmacopoeia*.

In 1939, a Tennessee company sold an anti-infective sulfa drug for children called Elixir Sulfanilamide. Unfortunately, it was formulated with an alcohol related to antifreeze and was never tested before marketing. Over 100 people died, many of whom were children. Public outcry again provided the impetus for a new law to regulate drugs, cosmetics and medical devices. It required that drugs be labelled with adequate directions for use, mandated safety to be established, prohibited false therapeutic claims and authorized factory inspections.

In response to the thalidomide disaster (thalidomide was a sedative that was approved and sold in Europe, but had not yet been approved for sale in the U.S.) which produced thousands of deformed new-borns outside the U.S., the law was amended in 1962 to require that both safety and efficacy had to be established before a drug could be approved and sold in the U.S. It also added stricter controls over clinical trials and established acceptable manufacturing practices for the drug industry and provided FDA additional powers to inspect manufacturing facilities. In addition, the new law required all antibiotics to be certified and gave FDA control of prescription drug advertising. As an interesting historical footnote, thalidomide was recently approved by the FDA to treat leprosy and is being used off-label for treatment of cancer.

Medical devices came under additional scrutiny in 1976 as the result of injuries to thousands of women caused by the Dalcon Shield intrauterine device (IUD). Thereafter, medical devices were subjected to more rigorous regulatory control.

In 1983, the Orphan Drug Act became law and was designed to promote development of products for rare diseases, defined as diseases with less than 200,000 patients in the U.S. The law provides a seven-year marketing exclusivity in the U.S. (10 years under comparable regulations in Europe and Japan) and a 50% tax credit for research expenses.

Also in 1983, the Bureau of Drugs merged with the Bureau of Biologics to form the National Center for Drugs and Biologics. In 1987, they were split into two divisions: the Center for Drug Evaluation and Research (CDER, pronounced "SEE-der") and the Center for Biologics Evaluation and Research (CBER, pronounced "SEE-ber"). Recently, they are in the process of coming closer together again administratively.

CURRENT FDA

OGD

In 1992, the Generic Drug Enforcement Act came into being and the Office of Generic Drugs (OGD) was formed as part of FDA. The OGD continues to have responsibility for approval of generic drugs.

PDUFA

Also in 1992, the Prescription Drug User Fee Act (PDUFA, pronounced "puh-DOO-fa") required drug and biologic manufacturers to pay fees to FDA for the evaluation of drug and biologic filings, currently $2.2 million in 2014, up from $1.4 million for a 2010 New Drug Application (NDA) filing. In addition there are annual fees required to be paid by brand drug manufacturers for each establishment ($555,000), a finished dosage form facility fee ($220,000), and product fees ($104,000) for each product including different dosage forms, etc... And you wondered why new branded drugs were expensive.

A 1997 amendment provided that small businesses got a break and owed no fee for their first filing of an NDA. If the filing is for a bioequivalence study only, the fee is cut in half. The user fees were intended to allow the hiring of more reviewers and thus speed new drug approvals. Against expectations, this has actually had its intended effect with the median time to approval cut in half from two years to one year.

A phrase you will hear from time to time is the "PDUFA date". That is the date the FDA is required by PDUFA to complete its review of an NDA and it is generally ten months following acceptance of the NDA by FDA. The FDA can reject or approve an NDA at that time, but if FDA does not approve the NDA, it will indicate what additional information the FDA requires to approve it. PDUFA also requires FDA to set out all of its requirements for approval on the PDUFA date and it may not sandbag, i.e., add new requirements in the future, unless there are special circumstances. In 2007, the PDUFA law was renewed for another five years. Under that legislation:

- FDA was granted additional authority to review direct-to-consumer ads (DTC) of the type common on TV today. First offense fines for false or misleading DTC ads are $250,000 with $500,000 per each subsequent violation.

- FDA may now deny a Citizen's Petition (CP) whose primary purpose is to delay approval of an ANDA if it does not raise valid scientific or regulatory issues. If a CP is filed and denied, the 30-month Hatch Waxman period is extended by any delay time, so that the 180-day first-filer generic exclusivity will not be lost while the FDA was considering a CP.

- FDA was granted the authority to provide a five year NCE exclusivity (instead of the three year new formulation exclusivity previously provided) for an isomer that was separated from an approved drug racemate, if the approval is for a new use, i.e., different therapeutic category, and the isomer cannot be approved for the same use as the racemate for ten years after its approval.

- FDA is authorized to charge user fees for filing for approvals of medical devices.

FDASIA

Under the FDA Safety and Innovation Act of 2012 (FDASIA), many more changes were made to both the Food and Drug Act governing drugs as well as the Public Health Service

Act governing biologics. In addition to reauthorizing PDUFA for another 5 years, it amends the Food and Drug Act to create new section 505E which grants an additional 5 years marketing exclusivity for drug products designated by FDA as a Qualified Infectious Disease Product ("QIDP"). A QIDP is defined as an antimicrobial drug for treating pathogens which pose a serious threat to public health.

That means that a drug designated as a QIDP would have 10 years exclusivity as an NCE, 8 years exclusivity for a new use or new formulation and 12 years for an orphan drug. Also, for NCEs, the time for filing an ANDA for a generic is also extended an additional 5 years (from 4 to 9 years after approval).

These new rules apply to drugs approved after July 9, 2012 and do not generally apply to improvements of previously approved drugs, but that is not entirely clear as with most new legislation. A drug sponsor may request FDA to designate its product a QIDP any time before the submission of an NDA. If granted, such drug will receive automatic priority review.

Biologically Derived Drugs

Biologically derived drugs (biologicals) are regulated under the Public Health Service Act of 1902 which provided pre-marketing approval originally for therapeutic agents of biological origin, such as vaccines and now of greater interest, biotech products. That means that drugs and biologicals are not regulated under the same statute. However, by and large, filings for approval of new biologicals, called Biological License Applications (BLAs), are evaluated in much the same manner as filings for approval of new drugs (New Drug Applications or NDAs) and the applicant must similarly establish safety and efficacy before its BLA will be approved.

One result of this difference is that while there are numerous generics of drugs, there are currently no generic biological products in the U.S. because technically until March, 2010, the Public Health Service Act did not provide for them. The Public

Health Service Act was amended in March, 2010 to provide for generic biologics, the so-called "biosimilars" and is discussed in more detail in Chapter 7.

OPDP

OPDP is the acronym for the Office of Prescription Drug Promotion, formerly called Division of Drug Marketing, Advertising and Communication (DDMAC). It reviews all promotional materials after approval and issues warning letters to the drug industry that number in the thousands annually. OPDP is the one that requires all the side effects warnings in TV ads and magazines that advertise drugs.

FDAMA

Recent developments include the Food and Drug Administration Modernization Act of 1997 (FDAMA pronounced "fa-DAH-ma", rhymes with "pajama"). This new law provides for pediatric exclusivity periods (see Chapter 5) and provides for dissemination of so-called off-label information from peer-reviewed journals. Generally speaking, a drug company is forbidden to promote a drug for any unapproved indication or off-label use. However, a doctor is legally allowed to use an approved drug to treat a patient for any indication he or she believes appropriate. Many drugs have significant off-label uses and that results in a conundrum for the drug companies and a goldmine for the federal government.

Washington Legal Foundation

The FDA insisted the drug companies could not say *anything* about off-label uses, including how to safely use its drugs for these off-label uses. This was a problem because doctors were using the drugs for off-label uses and the companies had no way of communicating to the doctor to insure that the drugs were being used safely.

A foundation called the Washington Legal Foundation (WLF) sued FDA on the grounds that this violated the first amendment of the U.S. Constitution by forbidding commercial speech. Court decisions favored the WLF view and as a result, the companies are now allowed to provide copies of peer-reviewed medical and scientific journal articles showing the results of clinical trials on off-label uses to doctors that request such information.

In a recent landmark decision, the U.S. Court of Appeals for the Second Circuit in *U.S. v. Caronia* (2nd Cir. 2012) agreed with WLF that the First Amendment broadly protects the right of individuals to speak truthfully about off-label uses of FDA-approved products, even in a commercial context. In *Caronia*, the 2nd circuit overturned a criminal conviction of a drug salesman alleged to have promoted an FDA-approved pharmaceutical for an off-label use (that is, a use not strictly conforming to the uses specified on the FDA-approved labelling). The decision of the government to abandon an appeal marked another victory for WLF, which played a lead role in overturning the conviction.

However, the government continues to successfully file both civil and criminal suits against drug companies for alleged off-label promotion and extracts huge fines (literally billions of dollars) from virtually all of them under settlements, for the reason that none of the companies are willing to go to the mat over it because if they are found guilty, the government can ban them from selling their drugs to Medicare patients.

FDA ORANGE BOOK

The FDA Orange Book is the name used to describe an FDA publication "Approved Drug Products and Therapeutic Equivalents" available on line at **www.fda.gov/cder/ob**. The basic purpose of the Orange Book is to list information covering the branded drug products. If a patent is listed in the Orange Book, a generic company is required to provide a patent certification as part of its

ANDA. The patent certification is a key element of the Hatch Waxman Act that is discussed in more detail in Chapter 6.

In the Orange Book the FDA lists all approved drugs, their dates of approval, for what indication or use for which they were approved (so-called "patent use code") and the dates and types of regulatory exclusivities that apply to those drugs, if any. It was originally called the Orange Book because years ago it was only available as a hard copy bound in an orange cover. Now it is a website, but the name has stuck. For further details about the Orange Book and how it relates to the Hatch Waxman Act, see Chapter 6.

DRUG INDUSTRY REGULATION

The FDA regulates the drug industry by requiring companies to obtain approval for major steps in the development of a drug and to establish that the drug is safe and effective for its intended use. In addition, the FDA oversees drug manufacturing and testing through the promulgation of lengthy and detailed written guidelines and procedures known as "Good Manufacturing Practices" (GMPs) and "Good Laboratory Practices" (GLPs). Current GMPs or GLPs are known as cGMPs and cGLPs.

Drug development is done in two broad phases known as pre-clinical and clinical. In pre-clinical development, the drug is tested in animals to establish safety. In clinical development, the drug is tested in humans to establish safety and efficacy.

Clinical Development: INDs and Phases I–IV

Clinical development is further broken down into five basic categories:

- Investigational New Drug (IND)
- Phase I

- Phase II

- Phase III

- Phase IV

The IND requires the sponsor to file for approval to start human testing after conducting suitable animal studies to demonstrate drug safety.

Phase I is testing in a small number of healthy human volunteers for safety.

Phase II is testing in a relatively small group of human volunteers with the disease or condition being treated for initial efficacy and for establishing the proper dose for the intended use of a new drug.

Phase III is testing in a large number of patients having the disease or condition for both safety and efficacy. The number of patients required varies with the use or indication for which the drug is being tested. That is, the number of patients in a Phase III study is selected to establish efficacy statistically and may vary from a few hundred to tens of thousands.

Phase IV is post-marketing studies approved by FDA to monitor long-term safety.

Well-controlled Studies

The FDA generally requires a minimum of two separate well-controlled Phase III studies in order to approve a new drug for market. A well-controlled study typically requires a double-masked, placebo-controlled study in which some patients receive drug and some receive a non-drug-containing imitation or placebo and neither the patient nor the doctor know which patient is receiving the drug and which patient is receiving the placebo. In order to obtain approval for a new drug, both studies must be clinically relevant and demonstrate that the drug is safe and statistically more efficacious than the placebo.

TYPES OF DRUG FILINGS

- NDA: New drugs are filed as a New Drug Application (NDA).

- ANDA: Generic drugs are filed as an Abbreviated New Drug Application (ANDA).

- Section 8 ANDA: An ANDA filing with labelling omitting an approved, but patented indication, enabling the ANDA filer to obtain approval for another non-patented approved indication for the reference drug. Section 8 filers do not have to provide a Paragraph IV certification and are not entitled to the first-filer 180-day exclusivity. This is the so-called "skinny" labelling or "carve-out". Section 8 filings are intended to get around a use patent for a second indication where the first indication is no longer patented. They are accepted by FDA so long as the safety of the drug is not compromised by the labelling omission.

- Paper NDA: Generic drugs may also be filed as a so-called "paper NDA" under a section of the regulations known as 505(b)(2) in which a drug formulation is approved, at least in part, on the basis of studies not conducted by the applicant and for which the applicant does not have a right of reference. Studies referred to may be described in public literature or in one or more approved applications. Thus a 505(b)(2) filing is essentially a hybrid between an NDA and an ANDA, in which approval may be based on new clinical studies and/or previous approvals. It is often used by companies seeking to reformulate existing products to avoid patent infringement. The Hatch Waxman exclusivities provided for 505(b)(2) approvals are the same as for NDAs, which is another reason a company might prefer such a filing type over an ANDA which is entitled to no exclusivities other than the 180 days for the first-filer patent challenger. It is also subject to the same litigation procedures as ANDAs under the Hatch Waxman Act, covered in Chapter 6.

• Suitability petitions: Applicants may seek approval of generics that differ in dosage strength from previously approved brand drugs. For example, if 50 and 100 mg tablets are already approved, one can ask the FDA via a suitability petition to approve a 75 mg generic tablet. The drawback of such a petition is it becomes public and anyone can take advantage of its approval, and it often takes a long time to get approved.

• BLA: New biologicals, products that are derived from biological processes and which use molecular biology and recombinant technology, are filed as a Biological License Application (BLA) and have separate regulations and approval standards.

Recall that one very important distinction between NDAs and BLAs is that until 2010, there were no laws in the U.S. that allowed generics to be filed for drugs approved as BLAs. However, in 2006, the FDA approved Sandoz' 505(b)(2) filing for human growth hormone called *Omnitrope*, the first biosimilar approved in the U.S. following its previous approval by the European Union a few months earlier. Details on the current state of generic biologics are discussed in Chapter 7.

ANDA Filing Backlog

In fiscal 2013 the FDA had a backlog of nearly 3,000 generic applications, compared to 780 at the end of 2005 and the median time for approval was over 30 months, up from 17 months in 2003. Under a new approach, the FDA said it would review generic applications based on whether the application is for a copy of a branded drug whose patent has expired or is near expiring. Within this group, further priority will be given to first-filer generics, meaning the first copies of a branded drug for which there are no generics approved.

The lengthening time for ANDA approvals is potentially a big problem for generics. Under the Hatch Waxman Act, as discussed in more detail in Chapter 6, the first generic filer who challenges a patent is entitled to a 180-day period of exclusivity, but can forfeit that exclusivity if its ANDA is not approved within 30 months of filing. Under the recent FDASIA legislation, the 30 month rule has been modified to allow more time in view of this backlog.

Accelerating NDA Approvals

The FDA also provides for three approaches to accelerate NDA approvals known as "fast track", "accelerated approval" and "priority review".

Fast track is intended to facilitate review of drugs to treat serious diseases and fill unmet medical needs. It typically provides eligibility for accelerated approval, rolling review and priority review and allows more communication with FDA. Rolling review allows an applicant to submit some of its required clinical data after filing its NDA, which allows one to file the NDA sooner and get earlier approval.

Accelerated approval allows for approval based on surrogate endpoints rather than clinical outcomes, which take longer to establish. Surrogate endpoints are those that are predictive of a clinical benefit such as tumor shrinkage in the case of a cancer drug. In addition, the applicant must agree to conduct Phase IV studies after approval to verify the anticipated clinical benefit such as extending survival time.

Priority review is for drugs that offer the potential to provide significant improvement over marketed products in the same class, such as increased efficacy or substantial reduction of side effects. Drugs eligible for priority review have a six month review in place of the normal ten month review cycle. FDA grants priority review within 45 days of filing a request for it.

An example of accelerated approval that did not come out as well as expected is Avastin, a Roche/Genentech anti-cancer drug. As reported in the Wall Street Journal in December, 2010, Avastin is approved for treatment of several types of tumors including lung and colon cancer. In 2008, the FDA gave Avastin accelerated approval for use in the treatment of metastatic breast cancer on the condition that additional studies were carried out to confirm the initial trial. The new studies indicated that Avastin did not extend patients' lives overall, nor did it inhibit tumor growth enough to outweigh the harmful side effects seen in the additional trials. As a result, the FDA has recommended that its prior approval for this use should be cancelled.

MEDICAL DEVICES

FDA also regulates medical devices as outlined in the Code of Federal Regulations (21 CFR 800). Medical devices are divided into three classes. Class I relates to simple medical devices which present minimal potential for harm to the user, such as tongue depressors. Class III relates to devices that sustain or support life or are implanted, such as heart valves. Class II medical devices are those that fall in between such as home pregnancy kits.

Class I devices require no testing, but are subject to general controls such as meeting GMPs.

Class II devices are also subject to general controls and also "special controls", such as performance standards, post-market surveillance and other regulations.

Class III devices are the most regulated and require one of two forms of pre-market approval: a Pre-market Notification

(PMN, also known as the section 510K process) or a Pre-market Approval (PMA). Class III devices can only use the PMN process if the manufacturer can establish that its device is "substantially similar" to an earlier device that was marketed before 1976. As a result, new Class III devices must be filed as PMAs and require proof of safety and efficacy, much as a new drug.

The initial FDA filing for a Class III device is called an Investigational Device Exemption (IDE) that allows human testing much as an IND allows human testing for drugs. Under the applicable statute, FDA has six months to review a PMA after it is filed. The FDA also may require the manufacturer to comply with certain post-approval obligations.

Under the PMN process, the FDA may allow subsequent manufacturers to file a submission under section 510K of the regulations for Class II devices. If they can establish their product is "substantially similar" to the approved medical device, they can obtain "clearance" by the FDA to market their device. The "clearance" is not technically an approval, so those companies cannot say that they are "FDA approved". Nonetheless, the 510K clearance is a convenient and much less expensive shortcut to marketing a Class II device since no data on safety and efficacy is required.

ANTIBIOTICS

Before 1997 antibiotics were not approved as NDAs, but instead were approved under FDCA section 507. For this reason, antibiotics were excluded from the Hatch Waxman Act, and these so-called "old antibiotics" that had been filed prior to November 20, 1997, were ineligible for Orange Book listing, 30-month stays, market exclusivities, etc.

In 1997 the FDA Modernization Act repealed section 507 and brought antibiotics into the NDA process under section 505 and therefore antibiotics are now subject to the provisions of the Hatch Waxman Act, including patent certifications and exclusivity. In addition, the Q1 Act of 2008 applied the three-year exclusivity and Orange Book rules (patent listing, certification, carve outs, etc.) to old antibiotics, so that now antibiotics are essentially treated the same as conventional drugs.

DRUG AGENCIES OUTSIDE THE U.S.

Europe

The drug agency for Europe corresponding to FDA is the European Medicines Agency (EMA). The EMA uses a so-called "centralized procedure" in which there is a single review by all countries at one time and the approval is for all countries or none. The NDA there is called a Marketing Authorization Application (MAA). The current cost for submission of a MAA is Euro 267,000 plus Euro 25,000 for each additional dosage form, with discounts available for small companies and for orphan drugs filings. The EMA receives over 100 applications annually.

There is also another procedure called the Mutual Recognition Procedure (MRP) in which you start with one country known as the Reference Member State (RMS). When the RMS approves your product, you can move on to other countries, called Concerned Member States (CMS), to get their approvals. I mention these details just to give you a flavor of what appears to be bureaucracy gone wild. One almost expects to run across a specialized veterinary agency called AE-ROUS (with apologies to the movie *The Princess Bride*) short for Agency for Evaluation of Rodents of Unusual Size.

The EMA is also responsible for managing parallel imports of pharmaceutical products from one country in Europe to another. This is known as parallel trade. The way this works, for example, is when a company sells its drug product in Spain, a low-priced country for drugs, the drugs are re-imported by third parties back to the higher-priced European countries and sold again at higher prices, similar in principle to the proposed re-importation of U.S. drug products from Canada to the U.S.

In the European Union (EU), a union of 27 European countries, patents will not prevent this on the theory of exhaustion of patent rights and the free movement of goods throughout the EU. That is, once a patented drug product is sold inside the EU, its patent rights are lost and may not be used to prevent re-importation to another member country of the EU, so long as the patent owner or one in concert with him made the first sale.

There is one exception to this rule which applies to the 10 new, mostly Eastern European countries that joined the EU on May 1, 2004 including Poland, the Czech Republic, Slovenia, Slovakia, Hungary, etc. For these countries, if the patent owner could not have obtained a patent in one of those countries due to the fact that pharmaceutical products were not patentable at the time of filing of the patents for the product in Europe, then parallel imports from that country are not allowed.

Pharmaceutical companies in Europe have tried to fight parallel trade, but with limited success. It is a form of generic competition, but with insult added to injury in that the parallel importers are selling *your own product* in competition with you. According to PharmaTimes, some 140 million packs of medicines are parallel traded in Europe every year. Companies such as Pfizer have been vocal in opposition to parallel trade in the past, claiming that not only does it affect sales, but the fragmented and often untraceable supply routes of parallel-traded drugs opens up the supply chain to infiltration of counterfeit medicines. Some companies instituted programs to limit sales of products to those distributors who cooperated with parallel importers and the EU took the position that this was illegal anti-competitive behavior.

In 2008 three big pharma companies, Pfizer, J&J and Bayer, won an important parallel trade case in Brussels which allowed them to stop supplying the Belgian company Bofar, reportedly one of the countries' largest parallel distributors, with medicines. That has given pharmaceutical companies in Europe something to work with, but parallel imports continue to be problems for them since prices for the same products vary by country, based partially on differing governmental pricing requirements, but also on significant differences in the cost of living in member countries.

Japan

The Japan Health Ministry is called the Ministry of Health, Labor and Welfare (MHLW). The equivalent of their FDA was reorganized as of April 1, 2004 and now is called the Pharmaceutical and Medical Devices Agency (PMDA). It combined three previous agencies responsible for assessment and approval of drugs and medical devices into one agency, including KIKO, the one responsible for advising on clinical trials. Since 2008, the PMDA has greatly expanded and has reduced approval times and increased the number of approvals. Average time for approval in Japan was 32 months in 1996, but is now comparable to the shorter approval times in the U.S. (12 months) and in Europe (16 months).

Japan has an interesting approach to minimizing issues about generics. When a drug is approved, it is assigned a reimbursement price by another government agency (the NHI price) and the government reimburses patients for the drug based on that price. The initial price of the drug tends to be high by U.S. standards. But every two years, the government lowers the NHI price on the majority of prescription drugs in the range of 4–6%. Over the normal lifetime of a drug, the NHI price of the drug drops significantly and by the time the patents and any regulatory exclusivity have expired, the price is already so low there is not much incentive for generics to enter the market.

This constant price reduction is taking its toll on the health of the Japanese pharmaceutical industry and may encourage consolidation of companies in Japan at some point. Realizing this pricing policy was not healthy for its national pharma industry as a whole, Japan is now reviewing its pricing system. Under a one year pilot program in 2013, the price of newly approved medicines will be maintained during the life of the patent.

Japan does provide for generics, but has an interesting way of assigning prices for them. The first generic of a branded drug to be approved gets an NHI price of 90% of the NHI price for the branded drug. The second generic to be approved is priced at 80% of the NHI price for the branded drug, etc. And every two years the prices for generics are also cut as their branded counterparts. Generics represent less than 20% of prescriptions in Japan as doubt over the safety and quality of generic drugs remains an issue among the dispensing pharmacies. New prescription forms introduced in 2008 now allow for generic substitution if the doctor does not expressly forbid it and the government has promised a financial premium to pharmacies that dispense at least 30% of prescriptions as generics.

An additional change of interest is the Pharmaceuticals Affairs Law that was amended in 2002 to add "distribution approval" to "manufacturing approval". This means a company may seek approval of a drug without having to have its own manufacturing plant in Japan and may use contract manufacture for the approved product which was not allowed before. Also to be added is the system of using Drug Master Files (DMFs) to protect the intellectual property of bulk drug manufacturers, as is common in the U.S.

TAKE HOME MESSAGE

• The U.S. Food and Drug Administration (FDA) regulates the U.S. drug industry. In Europe, its counterpart is called the European Medicines Agency (EMA) and in Japan, the Pharmaceutical and Medical Devices Agency (PMDA).

- Clinical drug development consists of five phases: preclinical Investigational New Drug (IND) and Clinical Phases I-IV, all of which are closely monitored by FDA.

- Applications for approval of new drugs are filed as New Drug Applications (NDAs).

- Applications for approval of generic drugs are filed as Abbreviated New Drug Applications (ANDAs) or 505(b)(2)s.

- Applications for approval of biologically derived drugs are filed as Biological License Applications (BLAs).

- Applications for approval of Class III devices are filed as Premarket Approvals (PMAs) or 510Ks.

- The FDA Orange Book is where approved drugs products are listed, together with any patents and patent use codes and any regulatory exclusivities for branded drugs.

The next Chapter discusses **Drug Product Exclusivity**.

Chapter 5

Drug Product Exclusivity

EXCLUSIVITY OF DRUG PRODUCTS GENERALLY

Drug products have a number of different ways to obtain and
maintain exclusivity. In this context, exclusivity means that the
manufacturer retains exclusive rights to his drug product and no
third party is entitled to copy it and thereby take market share
through reduced prices. The basic exclusivities available are patent and regulatory and to a lesser extent trademarks and trade
dress.

PATENT EXCLUSIVITY

The most obvious exclusivity is by way of patents. A drug manufacturer will try to obtain one or more patents on the new chemical entity (NCE), and close relatives of it such as its salts, esters,
polymorphs such as hydrates and isomers and other chemical
forms of an NCE, alternative methods of manufacture, its formulation as an oral, topical or parenteral drug product, its use to treat
a disease or condition, novel dosage forms or dosage regimens,
combinations with other active drugs, new uses of treatment,
new conditions of use, etc. Patents can be obtained throughout

the life of an active drug and used to help maintain exclusivity. Patents on new combinations, new uses, new dosage forms and improved formulations are especially useful for this purpose.

REGULATORY EXCLUSIVITY

There are seven basic regulatory exclusivities for conventional drugs (as opposed to regulatory exclusivities for biologics, which are covered separately in Chapter 7) available under current U.S. law and regulations. They are:

1. Five year new chemical entity (NCE) exclusivity

2. Three year new condition of use or new indication exclusivity

3. Three year new formulation exclusivity

4. Seven year orphan drug exclusivity

5. Six month pediatric exclusivity

6. 180-day generic product exclusivity for the "first-filer" generic company under the Hatch Waxman Act

7. Five year added period for a Qualified Infectious Disease Product (QIDP)

The following are details of the seven U.S. regulatory exclusivities from longest to shortest:

Orphan Drug Exclusivity

The "orphan" drug exclusivity in the U.S. is for seven years marketing exclusivity and prevents the FDA from approving a third party NDA or BLA (Biological License Application) as well as an ANDA or paper NDA for the same active drug or biologic for the same orphan indication during the seven-year period. In short, the orphan drug exclusivity blocks approval of applications for the same active drug for the same medical indication. A second product may be approved if it uses a different drug chemically or if it is clinically superior, offers greater safety or is a major contribution to patient care.

To be eligible for orphan drug exclusivity, the drug product must be designated as an orphan drug by the FDA on the grounds that it is unprofitable or that it is for a disease or condition that affects less than 200,000 people in the U.S. and it must be the first designated drug to be approved for the orphan indication. Note that there is no restriction on *filing* an NDA or ANDA for an orphan drug before the seven-year period expires in contrast to the rule for NCE exclusivity.

Companies have used the Orphan Drug exclusivity as part of an overall plan to get an initial indication approved for the drug with future plans to extend the label indications. This is common for cancer drugs since the FDA requires proof of safety and efficacy for each type of cancer and oncologists commonly use cancer drugs off-label for other cancers.

The FDA recently amended its 1992 regulations for orphan drugs, effective August 12, 2013.

New Chemical Entity (NCE) Exclusivity

The law provides five years of marketing as well as data exclusivity in the U.S. from the date of approval of a drug containing an NCE. The five-year marketing exclusivity means that FDA will not approve an ANDA (or comparable paper NDA filed under 505(b)(2)) containing the same NCE for the same approved use for five years from the date of approval. The FDA may however approve an NDA for the same drug product.

The five-year data exclusivity means that the FDA will not accept an ANDA (or paper NDA) filing until the end of the fifth year, unless a patent is listed in the FDA "Orange Book", in which case the FDA will accept such a filing one year earlier, i.e., at any time after the end of the fourth year from marketing approval. This is highly significant as the mean time for approval of an ANDA is currently about 30 months, giving an effective marketing exclusivity of about 6.5 years rather than 5 years. If there is no patent, an ANDA cannot be filed before the end of the 5th year and with the current 30-month average approval time, the effective exclusivity would be about 7.5 years.

However FDA regulations seem to zero out that difference. If a generic company files an ANDA and Paragraph IV certification and notice between the end of the 4th year and before the end of the 5th year for a patented approved drug product with a five-year exclusivity, and the approved drug product owner files suit within 45 days of such notice, FDA regulations say that FDA will not approve the generic product until 7.5 years after its original approval, unless the patent is held invalid or unenforceable before the end of that time period (CFR 314.107).

Therefore an NCE should expect to receive a minimum of about 7.5 years of exclusivity, unless there is an early negative court ruling. This suggests that if a brand company has a patent for an NCE with a life of less than about 6 years from the date of approval, it might consider disclaiming the patent and not filing it in the Orange Book and simply rely on its regulatory exclusivity, which is more reliable than a patent and requires no expense for enforcement, and that would also deprive a first-filer of its 180-day exclusivity.

The five-year exclusivity applies only to the first approval of an NCE in any drug product in the U.S. That is, if a second drug product for another use or indication containing that same NCE is filed by the same or different manufacturer, there is no second five-year exclusivity allowed, even if the first drug product has been withdrawn or was never sold or the second drug product is in a completely different form for a completely different use, as long as the first drug product containing the same NCE was previously approved.

New Condition of Use or New Indication or New Formulation Exclusivity

The law provides marketing exclusivity of three years for a new condition of use or new indication or new formulation. This exclusivity applies to new indications or new conditions of use for an old drug or new formulations or other labelling changes of an old drug for which the applicant has submitted and obtained approval of a new NDA and which required new clinical trials (but not bioavailability studies) funded by the sponsor of the NDA that were essential to obtain approval.

The new indication can involve the same or a different formulation or dosage as long as it is for a new use of an old drug product or involves a change in the conditions of use of an old drug product. During those three years, the FDA will not approve an ANDA (or paper NDA) for that new indication or condition of use. However, the FDA will accept the filing of an ANDA (or paper NDA) during the three-year period and thus the ANDA theoretically could be approved by the end of the third year. The FDA will also approve a new NDA during the three-year period; however, it is unlikely that anyone would attempt to prepare and file a full NDA for the same indication since they would only have to wait for three years to copy it with an ANDA filing and preparing and filing a full NDA would take longer and cost much more.

One can also get the three-year exclusivity for the same product for the same indication based only on obtaining a new condition of use or other significant change in labelling. For example, a product labelled for twice-a-day use can get the three-year exclusivity if it is subsequently approved for use as a once-a-day treatment, assuming all the other requirements are met. This could be a good strategy for a quick short term fix since the twice-a-day generic could not be substituted at the pharmacy level for the once-a-day version of the same drug for the same use, without permission of the doctor.

Pediatric Exclusivity

The pediatric exclusivity adds six months marketing exclusivity to *all* the other exclusivities for the approved active drug as well as effectively adding six months to the expiration dates of any patents listed for the drug product in the Orange Book. While the patent terms are not actually extended, the FDA acts as if they were and will not approve ANDAs (or paper NDAs) until the extended date is met. The award of six months applies only to unexpired patents and exclusivities at the time the pediatric exclusivity is granted. The pediatric exclusivity applies to the active drug moiety, so that a related product or improved product containing the same active drug moiety also receives the pediatric extension if it was approved at the time the pediatric exclusivity was awarded.

A pediatric exclusivity is possible only if the FDA makes a request for a clinical study to be done in children and that it is done in accordance with FDA's instructions. The study does not need to be successful in order to be eligible for the six-month exclusivity. If an ANDA has been submitted and is ready for approval after the pediatric study has been submitted to FDA, but before FDA has accepted it, FDA may hold up the ANDA approval for up to 90 days while it is reviewing the submission for approval. Under a new statute, the FDA can now require NDA holders to perform pediatric studies.

180-Day Generic Product Exclusivity

Under current law, the first generic drug manufacturer to file a substantially complete ANDA for a drug product listed in the

Orange Book and who also challenges at least one listed patent in the Orange Book for that drug product by filing what is called a Paragraph IV certification is eligible for a 180-day exclusivity period. During that 180-day period the FDA may not approve another ANDA for the same drug product for the same indication.

There are also statutory ways in which the 180-day exclusivity can be forfeited or blunted through what are called "authorized generics" which are generic products authorized by the branded company which compete with the first-filer generic company, effectively robbing them of their 180-day exclusivity. The 180-day generic product exclusivity is covered in more detail in Chapter 6 under the Hatch Waxman Act.

Five Year Add-on for Qualified Infectious Disease Products

The FDA Safety and innovation Act of 2012, discussed in the previous chapter on FDA, created new Section 505E which adds five years of marketing exclusivity upon approval of an NDA for a drug product designated by FDA as a Qualfied Infectious Disease Product ("QIDP"). A QIDP is defined as an antimicrobial drug for treating pathogens which pose a serious threat to public health. Under this new law for so-called "QIDPs", the 5 year NCE exclusivity becomes 10 years; the 3 year exclusivity for a new condition of use or new indication or new formulation becomes 8 years and the 7 year orphan exclusivity becomes 12 years. The QIDP add-on also applies to the pediatric exclusivity which would mean a QIDP orphan drug could have the longest exclusivity for a conventional drug of 12.5 years (7 plus 5 plus 0.5).

In addition, for a QIDP with NCE exclusivity, the data exclusivity period, during which an ANDA with a Paragraph IV certification to an Orange Book listed patent on the QIDP cannot be submitted, is also extended by 5 years (from 4 years after NDA approval to 9 years after approval), giving such an NCE

QIDP an effective exclusivity of 11.5 years with the 30 month automatic stay following suit.

Other Exclusivities

Other common forms of exclusivity are trade dress, trademarks and trade secrets. Of these, the most common for pharmaceuticals is trade dress in the form of tablet shape, size and color.

Generally trade dress refers to the non-functional appearance of a product or its packaging including the shape or design of the product itself. If a trade dress also satisfies the requirements for trademark protection, it can be trademarked as well. One example would be the glass bottle used for many years by Coca Cola. Its unique shape acquired distinctiveness and became associated with the source of the product and therefore could be trademarked and Coke could prevent other soft drinks from using it.

A number of courts have found that the color, size and shape of pharmaceutical tablets are arbitrary and non-functional having nothing to do with the product's therapeutic function and therefore may be protected as trade dress if they become distinctive. However, a more recent case (*Shire v. Barr*, Fed. Cir. 2003) found that providing similar, but not identical color and shape for drug tablets to treat hyperactivity improved patient acceptance and compliance thereby making them functional and not protectable as trade dress.

Barr used similar, but not identical shapes and colors for its generic tablets and also used a "b" mark on each tablet, while Shire used the letters AD for Adderall, the brand name of the product. This case suggests that relying on color and shape for distinctiveness and exclusivity is not likely to offer strong protection in the future, except possibly to prevent virtually identical copying of nonfunctional color, shape and marking, which could lead to claims of unfair competition by passing off the generic company's tablets as the innovator's.

Trademarks can also offer some protection for prescription drug products over time, especially famous ones such as Viagra or Botox. These drug trademarks cannot become generic for a product because the FDA will not allow a generic company to use a trademark to name the generic drug product. The generic product must be named according to the drug's authorized non-proprietary name which is established by the International Non-proprietary Name (INN) or the U.S. Adopted Name (USAN) organizations.

The FDA also will not let another company use a confusingly similar trademark to yours for its product. In this regard, the FDA functions as a mini-trademark office to insure that there will be no incorrectly prescribed drugs because of confusingly similar trademarks. As a result, the FDA pays special attention to the initial letters of a trademark as physicians' writing clarity is famous for its absence in a typical prescription order form. As a result, brand name companies typically apply for multiple trademarks for their products before approval, so they will be sure to have at least one the FDA will accept.

EXCLUSIVITY OUTSIDE THE U.S.

Many countries are more liberal with regulatory exclusivities. In Europe, the current EU directive (regulation 727/2004) provides for a total of ten years of exclusivity for a new chemical entity (NCE) filed after November 1, 2005, but not for improvements of old drugs or for new uses of old drugs. Under a ruling by the European Court of Justice in a case brought by Novartis to obtain exclusivity for an improved version of one of its older products, the Court ruled that the previous law provided no exclusivity for improvements to drug products. New NCEs filed after November 1, 2005 are eligible for this exclusivity if they use the centralized procedure.

Under the old rules for drugs filed in Europe prior to November 1, 2005, exclusivity for NCEs is ten years for centrally filed drugs and six or ten years for drugs filed one country at a time under the MRP procedure. The six-year countries comprise the mostly smaller countries (Austria, Denmark, Finland, Greece, Ireland, Iceland, Norway, Portugal and Spain); the ten-year countries comprise the mostly larger ones (France, Germany, Italy, U.K., Sweden, Holland, Belgium and Luxembourg). As a practical matter, regulatory exclusivity for many older approved drugs in Europe is still governed by the old rules.

Under current EU regulations, a new chemical entity or NCE will receive eight years of data exclusivity plus two additional years of marketing exclusivity plus one additional year of marketing exclusivity based on approval of an improvement if it involves a "significant new indication". The additional year attaches to both the improvement and the original product only if the improvement product is approved within eight years of approval of the original product. This means that a generic cannot be filed until the end of the data exclusivity period of eight years and it can't be sold until the end of the additional two or three year marketing exclusivity.

While this may be okay for the original product, it provides limited exclusivity for the improvement. If the new indications are not deemed "significant", the one-year exclusivity applies only to the improvement. Thus it is clear that the EU has made a policy decision not to encourage improvements of pharmaceutical products, but instead to favor generics of older products. There is also a one year exclusivity for switches to OTC status from a well-recognized prescription product, which is intended to encourage OTC switches, since the government does not reimburse OTC drugs. There is also a ten-year exclusivity for orphan drugs that is an important regulatory exclusivity.

Another related issue is when a generic company may start to do the work required to obtain approval without infringing patents covering the drug. This is the so-called "Bolar Provision" which is named after a famous early 1980s U.S. lawsuit,

Roche v. Bolar, which held that a generic company could *not* start work on a generic product while a relevant patent was still in force. This lead to the passing of the Hatch Waxman Act in 1984, which is discussed in Chapter 6, which changed the law to allow generics to work on developing generic products prior to patent expiration without fear of being sued for patent infringement.

In Europe EU Directive 2004/27 has a provision which allows studies and trials to be undertaken without infringement of patent rights. As a result, generic companies may start studies and clinical trials while patents covering the product are still in force without infringing them, and the generic products may be approved and commercially sold the same day the patent expires.

In 2007, new EU legislation on medicines for children entered into force. It generally provides a six-month extension of exclusivity, as in the U.S., but also provides for an additional two-year extension of market exclusivity for pediatric orphan drugs. The new regulations also provide ten years exclusivity for old drugs without patent protection that are developed exclusively for use in children and the company developing the new pediatric product can use the same brand name for the corresponding product approved for adults.

Therefore the longest non-patent conventional drug product exclusivity in Europe is for a pediatric version of an orphan drug and that is 12 years. Therefore, a good drug development strategy for the EU would be to identify such an orphan drug candidate and develop it for adults and children. That is not as hard as it might appear as many very specific diseases and conditions affect only a limited population and it is likely that, once the drug is approved for that orphan use, it will receive off-label use for related conditions. That is a common tactic used by companies in the cancer field who obtain approval for a rare cancer and that allows doctors to use the drug for related cancers.

Japan provides 4–10 years of data exclusivity: six years for NCEs, recently extended to eight years, four years for improvements and ten years for orphan drugs. In addition, generics must also obtain pricing approval from the National Health Insurance (NHI), so-called "NHI price", as well as market approval and this adds additional exclusivity time.

Since 2002, China has provided six years; New Zealand five years, but only for new NCEs; and Australia five years. Canada provided no effective regulatory exclusivity until 2006. Under new regulations effective for drugs approved after June 17, 2006, there is now eight years of exclusivity available for innovative drugs containing an NCE, consisting of six years of data exclusivity and two years of marketing exclusivity.

India's drug industry has an unusual history. Before 2005, pharmaceutical patents were not recognized. That encouraged a growing and successful generic drug industry. After joining the World Trade Organization (WTO) India had to change its patent policy, but did so with an eye on protecting that industry. For example, the law bars patents for minor improvements to existing drugs, such as re-formulations of old drug products, a practice sometimes referred to as "evergreening". In addition, India's laws also provide for compulsory licensing to force a firm to license its patented drug to a local generic company. And a government committee in India concluded in 2007 after three years of deliberation that it may not be in India's national interest to grant data exclusivity for pharmaceuticals, despite the requirements of international law.

Those requirements are set forth in the World Trade Organization's "Agreement on Trade Related Aspects of Intellectual Property Rights" (TRIPS). Article 39.3 of TRIPS provides that countries must protect against unfair commercial use of confidential data on new chemical entities submitted by companies to obtain approval for marketing new drugs from a regulatory agency. As of 2013, India still had no data protection for pharmaceuticals.

TAKE HOME MESSAGE

• There are seven regulatory exclusivities, including the new QIDP add- on, for conventional drugs in the U.S.:

1.	Orphan drug:	7 years
2.	New Chemical Entity (NCE):	5 years
3.	New indication *or* condition of use:	3 years
4.	New formulation:	3 years
5.	Pediatric:	6 months
6.	First-to-file generic exclusivity:	180 days
7.	QIDP add on:	5 years

• First-filer generic exclusivity is a significant incentive for generic companies to seek to invalidate patents covering innovative drugs, but it can also be forfeited or reduced in value by authorized generics.

• Exclusivities for Europe: New drug Applications (NCEs) filed for approval before November 1, 2005 have exclusivity of ten years for centrally filed drugs, or six or ten years for filings under the MRP procedure. NCEs filed after November, 2005 get 10–11 years of exclusivity, 10 years for orphan drugs, 12 years for pediatric orphan drugs, one year for new uses or OTC switches and 6 months additional exclusivity for pediatric use. No exclusivity is provided for improved formulations or new uses of old drugs.

• Exclusivities for Asia: Japan provides 6 (recently increased to 8) years of exclusivity for NCEs, 4 years for certain improvements and 10 years for orphan drugs; New Zealand and Australia 5 years for NCEs; China 6 years for NCEs; India nada, none, zip, zero.

- Exclusivity for Canada: 8 years for NCE's approved after June 17, 2006 consisting of 6 years data exclusivity and 2 years marketing exclusivity.

The previous chapters have discussed patents and FDA and regulatory exclusivity. The next Chapter discusses the **Hatch Waxman Act**. This law is the third leg of the life-cycle management stool and integrates the two separate disciplines of patents and regulatory into one interrelated discipline.

Chapter 6

Hatch Waxman Act

HISTORICAL BACKGROUND

The Hatch Waxman Act was enacted in 1984 as a result of a tacit agreement between the established innovator drug industry and an emerging generic drug industry to solve both of their problems. The generic industry was unhappy because a recent court decision, *Roche v. Bolar*, had established that a generic company could be sued for patent infringement for doing the testing necessary to file an ANDA before the patent expired, so that patent terms were being effectively extended, since it takes two to three years to do the required testing and obtain approval, and that would now all have to be done after patent expiration.

On the other hand the innovator companies were unhappy because regulatory requirements were taking longer and longer to meet and significant portions of the patent life of the drugs were being lost. And Congress wanted to make available cheaper forms of drugs that were no longer covered by patent and wanted to overrule the *Bolar* decision.

So the industries and Congress hit upon a compromise which would allow the generic industry to be able to do the testing while the patent was still in force so they could sell generic products the day the patent expired. In exchange, the innovator companies would be able to get the terms of their patents extended to make up for some of the patent term lost because of the required regulatory testing for approval. In addition, the generic industry would be able to rely on the safety and efficacy data for the drug product filed with the FDA by the innovator, so long as it could establish they were the same as the innovator drug.

The new law also gave the generic industry the opportunity to challenge the innovator's patents prior to going on the market to avoid the risk of payment of significant damages if the patent was upheld. At the same time, it also allowed the innovators to keep generic products off the market while the patent was being tested in court and off the market until the patent expired if it was upheld.

Henry Waxman, Democratic Congressman from California, and Oren Hatch, Republican Senator from Utah, co-sponsored the non-contentious "Drug Price Competition and Patent Term Restoration Act of 1984" and both industries and Congress thought they got what they wanted. Now 30 years later, things are more contentious. In addition a number of changes to the law have recently been made.

THE LAW TODAY

Generally under Hatch Waxman, FDA will approve a generic drug in the form of an Abbreviated New Drug Application (ANDA) if the generic company establishes that its product is therapeutically equivalent, that is, both pharmaceutically equivalent and bioequivalent, to the drug it wants to copy.

"Pharmaceutically equivalent" means the generic drug contains the same active drug, uses the same dosage form and strength, and employs the same route of administration and has the same labelling as the innovator or "reference" drug.

"Bioequivalent" means that the generic drug will function in the body in the same way as the branded drug.

In order to be substitutable for a branded drug by a pharmacist, a generic company must prove to the FDA that its generic drug is therapeutically equivalent to the branded drug. If an ANDA drug is not found to be therapeutically equivalent, it can still be approved, but it will not be substitutable for the reference drug unless a doctor agrees.

For example, for tablets for oral use, one must establish dissolution times and blood levels of active drug after ingestion that are comparable to the branded drug, but no clinical trials are required. There are exceptions however, e.g., generic products for ophthalmic, otic (ear) and parenteral solutions can request a waiver of bioequivalence under FDA regulations, but other locally acting drugs typically require clinical testing in humans to establish therapeutic equivalence. This is an important difference as bioequivalency studies are typically expensive and time-consuming and generic companies do not like to do them if they can be avoided.

When a generic company files its ANDA, it must also make a patent certification if there are any patents covering the branded drug product listed in the Orange Book. As you may recall from Chapter 4 on the FDA, the Orange Book is where the innovator companies are required to list patents covering their branded drug products.

FDA ORANGE BOOK

The Orange Book is the place where the FDA lists all approved drugs, their dates of approval, for what indication or use which they have been approved (so-called "patent use code") and the dates and types of regulatory exclusivities that apply to those drugs. In addition the Orange Book lists the "therapeutic equivalence" for each approved generic drug, which determines whether the generic drug may be substituted at the pharmacy without physician approval. The law also requires the patent owner or drug approval owner to list certain types of patents that cover the approved drug in the Orange Book. The patent listings in the Orange Book trigger portions of the Hatch Waxman Act.

Patents Listed in the Orange Book

Types of patents which must be listed in the Orange Book are patents that claim the active drug in the drug product, the formulation of the drug product, an inactive ingredient or excipient present in the formulation or patents covering its approved indication or other conditions of use.

Patents relating to methods of manufacturing the active drug in the drug product may not be listed, but patents claiming novel active drug products claimed in product-by-process claims can be listed. (A product-by-process claim is one that claims a product by defining it in terms of the process by which it is made). Patents claiming metabolites of the active drug (i.e., compounds which are formed in the body by metabolic processes after the drug has been administered) or intermediates used in the manufacture of the active drug may not be listed. Packaging and container patents may not be listed. Patents claiming unapproved indications or uses may not be listed.

Patents for polymorphs (different physical forms of the active drug such as crystalline forms, waters of hydration, solvates and amorphous forms) that claim the same physical form as the approved drug product may be listed. However, polymorphs that contain a different physical form from the approved product may be listed only if the patent holder has data to demonstrate that the different polymorph is the "same" active substance (i.e., both pharmaceutically equivalent and bioequivalent) as the approved active drug.

The applicable statute requires that patents must be listed within 30 days of FDA approval of the drug product. If the patent is granted after approval of the drug product, it must be listed within 30 days of the patent grant. However, FDA regulations allow the FDA to list a patent submitted after this 30-day period, but an ANDA or paper NDA filed prior to the date of the late listing is not required to file a Paragraph IV certification for that late-listed patent. The patent owner may still sue the generic company on that patent, but the patent owner is not entitled to a 30-month stay for it. However, if there were one or more timely listed patents in the Orange Book, the patent owner would already have a 30-month stay in place, so he could simply add the new patent to the existing suit.

The Orange Book listing is made by FDA after receipt of form 3542 which provides the necessary patent information. Form 3542a is submitted by the patent owner with the NDA and form 3542 is submitted within 30 days of its approval. These forms are essentially identical except that 3542 requires that the patent owner for a method of use patent submit a description of the approved indication or method of use that the applicant proposes FDA use as the "Patent Use Code" in the Orange Book.

Patent Use Codes

The scope of the patent use code is important in one particular area of generics known as a Section 8 Statement which allows for so-called "skinny labelling" or "carve-outs". Normally, a generic product must have the same labelling as the brand product. An exception to this rule is when a use patent is listed in the Orange Book and the generic filer requests that the FDA approve an ANDA which omits the patented use in its labelling, which is allowed under FDCA section 505(j)(2)(A)(viii).

This has lead to litigation over the scope of the patent use code. Caraco, a generic drug company, filed a Section 8 ANDA for a labelled use not covered by Novo's patent use code listed in Novo's Orange Book filing. Unexpectedly, Novo then amended its patent use code by broadening it outside the scope of its patent in such a way that Caraco could no longer properly provide a labelled use that was not covered by the new use code. Caraco complained to the FDA, but FDA took the position that it was not responsible for determining the proper scope of Novo's use code.

In a then pending suit with Novo, Caraco counterclaimed to limit the scope of Novo's use code to the claims of Novo's use patent. The district court agreed with Caraco and ordered Novo to narrow its use code to the scope of the claims of its patent. Novo appealed and in *Novo Nordisk v. Caraco* (Fed. Cir. 2010), the Federal Circuit overruled the District Court and held that a generic company does not have a statutory basis to counterclaim for a change in a patent use code. The Court, recognizing that this left Caraco with no remedy, suggested that it was up to FDA or Congress to fix it.

Instead, the Supreme Court weighed in *Caraco v. Novo* (Supreme Court 2012) and overruled the Federal Circuit and held a generic manufacturer is entitled to counterclaim to force correction of a patent use code that inaccurately describes the brand's use patent. The Court held that a patent use code qualifies as "patent information" and may therefore be the subject of a counterclaim to correct or delete patent information as provided by the statute.

Therapeutic Equivalence

Another important piece of information listed in the FDA Orange Book for a generic product is its *therapeutic equivalence* (TE) rating. If a product has an "A" rating, it may be substituted at the pharmacy level for a branded drug without approval by the doctor prescribing the brand name drug. This is the most important rating a generic product can receive. If a generic product is "B" rated, it cannot be substituted for the brand drug without the doctor's permission.

Since the typical generic product is not promoted, not being "A" rated means it will likely not sell as doctors will know little about it and the pharmacist is not free to legally substitute it for the brand drug. "B" rated products can be sold of course, and they are typically sold as "branded generics" and are promoted to doctors and hospitals in the same way as branded drugs.

In order to be "A" rated by FDA, the FDA must make a determination based on scientific information provided by the generic company that the generic drug product is *therapeutically equivalent* to the branded drug product, i.e., that it is *pharmaceutically equivalent* (contains the same active ingredient(s), dosage form, strength or concentration and route of administration as the branded drug product) and *bioequivalent* (acts the same way as the branded drug product in the body).

A typical "A" rating for an oral dosage form such as a pill is "AB rated" which means the generic is bioequivalent and may be freely substituted for the brand drug. That typically means patient blood levels of the drug were found to be the same with the generic drug as the branded drug. Other generic drugs, such as solutions used in eye care and skin care, may also receive an A rating even though technically one cannot do the same kinds of studies required to establish blood level bioequivalence, since the active drugs for eye and skin care do not enter the bloodstream. These are rated AT for topical and are also freely substitutable at the pharmacy level.

180-Day Generic Product Exclusivity

The 180-day generic product exclusivity was originally intended to encourage patent challenges to listed drugs by giving challengers what was thought to be a modest incentive to invalidate any patent(s) covering the listed drug product and therefore compensate the generic company for its costs in invalidating an improperly granted patent.

In practice, this modest incentive has become the single most important motivator for the generic industry because the first generic drug on the market typically obtains and maintains the majority of sales of that product indefinitely and more importantly, the profit made during that first 180-day period often exceeds the profit made for the rest of the life of the generic product. The reason for this is that in the absence of competition from other generic drugs, the first generic company does not significantly lower the price of the innovator drug during the six months exclusivity period which results in huge profits based on the minimum investment required to copy the innovator.

As a result of this single incentive, the patents covering drug products in the U.S. are being challenged at the earliest possible time since only the first to file an ANDA with a Paragraph IV certification challenging a patent for the listed drug is eligible for the 180-day exclusivity. As a result, the validity of virtually all patented drugs is being challenged, not necessarily because they are not covered by meritorious patents, but only because that is the road to riches. Thus major generic companies have scores of such suits ongoing and generic companies rely on the law of averages—if you place enough bets, you are sure to win a few of them and the cost of each bet is relatively low while the payout is enormous, so the more bets the better the return. The innovators are fighting back with innovative strategies of their own and those strategies are further explained in Chapter 8 on life-cycle management.

How does one become eligible for the 180-day exclusivity? As mentioned earlier, under current law, the first generic drug manufacturer to file a substantially complete ANDA for a drug product listed in the Orange Book and who also challenges at least one listed patent in the Orange Book for that drug product by filing what is called a Paragraph IV certification is eligible for a 180-day exclusivity period. During that 180-day period the FDA may not approve another ANDA for the same drug product for the same indication.

In this context "same drug product" means the exact same drug product including dosage form so that an ANDA filed for a 5 mg tablet of a given drug product would only prohibit FDA from approving another ANDA during the 180-day period for the same 5 mg tablet and thus the FDA would be free to approve another company's ANDA for a 10 mg tablet of the same active drug for the same indication.

The 180-day period starts when the generic drug is first commercialized in the U.S. However, under current law, the 180-day exclusivity period can be forfeited for a number of reasons:

1. If the generic drug is not sold within 75 days after the ANDA is approved or within 30 months after the ANDA is filed, whichever is earlier, or within 75 days from a final decision that the patent is invalid or not infringed, it is forfeited.

2. If another ANDA applicant obtains a final judgment invalidating the challenged patent, the first ANDA applicant must begin commercial marketing within 75 days, or else it is forfeited.

3. If the ANDA applicant withdraws its ANDA, or amends or withdraws its Paragraph IV certification, it is forfeited.

4. If the ANDA applicant enters into an agreement with either the NDA holder or another generic company, which agreement is determined by the FTC or a court to be anticompetitive, it is forfeited.

5. If all the patents for the listed drug product expire before the generic is marketed, it is forfeited.

Some branded companies have attempted to defeat the 180-day exclusivity by failing to pay fees on the patent, which causes it to expire, or disclaiming the patent and/or delisting it from the Orange Book. The courts have responded to such cases by ruling that such activity may be effective to forfeit the 180-day exclusivity under number 5 above, but only if it is done prior to a generic filing its Paragraph IV notice. Once the ANDA has been filed and the company receives the paragraph IV notice, it cannot defeat the 180-day exclusivity by unilaterally doing away with its patent.

Interestingly, if an ANDA applicant forfeits his 180-day exclusivity, the second ANDA filer to meet all the requirements does *not* become eligible for the 180-day exclusivity. Also, if two ANDA filers for the same listed drug file on the same day, the FDA currently takes the position that both are "first to file" so that they would share the 180-day exclusivity.

A current practice of the smaller generic companies today is to "share" their 180-day exclusivity with a large generic company by having the large generic company manufacture and/or distribute the drug and the smaller one who has the 180-day exclusivity shares the profits. This has spawned a whole new business model for small development companies who can identify a suitable branded drug, copy it, seek to invalidate any patents covering it and if successful, share profits on the sale of the generic product with a larger generic company with full manufacturing and distribution capability.

The rule changes in the 180-day exclusivity brought about by the 2003 Medicare Act apply to ANDAs filed after December 8, 2003. For ANDAs filed on or before that date, the old rules apply. The one change that is retroactive makes clear which court decision triggers the exclusivity period (this was ambiguous under the old law). It is now a final decision by a District Court if there is no appeal or it is a final decision of the Court of Appeals for the Federal Circuit if it is appealed.

As a practical matter the 180-day exclusivity often in fact is not exclusive. That is because the owner of the listed or branded drug can license a so-called "authorized generic" to a generic company or to its own generic division to compete with the generic company who obtained the 180-day exclusivity. Because consumers now have more choices, all sellers of the product must lower prices to stay competitive.

Generic companies challenged this practice in the courts and before the FDA on the grounds that it defeated the purpose of the Hatch Waxman 180-day exclusivity. The FDA replied that authorized generics lower drug prices to consumers and therefore they are consistent with the intent and goals of the Hatch Waxman Act. (One could conclude from this that the generic companies' often stated belief in the value of competition and resulting lower prices for consumers is muted only when their own exclusivity is threatened.) In fact, just as the rise of generic drugs has increased competition and lowered drug prices to consumers, the rise of authorized generics has similarly provided lower cost drug products to consumers. More on authorized generics in Chapter 8.

PATENT CERTIFICATIONS

There are four different patent certifications that can be made and the ANDA filer must make one of the following four certifications in his ANDA with respect to the patent listings in the Orange Book:

- I that there is no patent information listed
- II that there is a listed patent, but it is expired
- III that the listed patent will expire on a stated date
- IV that the listed patent is invalid or will not be infringed

If the ANDA filer makes one of the first two certifications, FDA can approve the ANDA when it is ready to do so. If the

ANDA filer makes the third certification, the FDA provides a "tentative approval" of the generic drug that becomes effective on the day the patent expires. The fun starts when the generic company makes the so-called "Paragraph IV" certification. Under Hatch Waxman, submission of an ANDA with a Paragraph IV certification is an "artificial act of patent infringement" allowing for the early litigation of patent disputes.

If the ANDA filer makes a Paragraph IV certification, he must notify the patent owner(s) and the owner of the NDA for the drug product (which may or may not be the same person) within 20 days of written acceptance of the ANDA by the FDA, which usually takes 60–90 days after filing the ANDA, and provide a detailed statement of the factual and legal basis for its opinion that the patent is not valid and/or will not be infringed.

Generic companies must make sure their opinions are factually accurate and scientifically sound as a baseless noninfringement or invalidity opinion could be the basis for a claim for reimbursement of its attorney's fees by the brand company if the court makes such a finding. In that regard, significant changes or abandonment of the original Paragraph IV positions may provide evidence that such positions were baseless and made in bad faith.

SUITS FOLLOWING PATENT CERTIFICATION

The Hatch Waxman Act provides that the patent owner has the right to file suit in Federal Court against the ANDA filer for infringement of the patent if he does so within 45 days of receipt of the Paragraph IV certification. If suit is filed, the FDA is prevented by law from approving the ANDA for 30 months from the date of receipt of the notice by the patent owner and NDA owner. The 30-month period can be shortened if the Court rules that the patent is invalid or unenforceable in less than 30 months. It can also be lengthened if the Court deems it necessary. If the patent holder does not file suit within the 45-day period, the FDA may approve the generic product at any time.

The patent owner typically sues following receipt of the Paragraph IV certification to try to keep the infringing product off the market to avoid the risk of potential disruption in the marketplace, loss of its sales and earnings, lowered stock price and reductions in force that typically occur when a generic product replaces a significant branded product.

However, a patent owner might not sue *subsequent* ANDA filers if, for example, a settlement with the first ANDA filer delayed entry of the first-filer. Since subsequent filers cannot get final approval before the first-filer receives his 180-day exclusivity, not suing subsequent filers can be an effective way to keep subsequent filers out of the market, so long as the first-filer does not forfeit its 180-day exclusivity. Subsequent filers know this of course and may respond to not being sued by filing a declaratory judgment action against the patent owner to try to invalidate the patent, which if successful may result in the first-filer forfeiting its 180-day exclusivity and the subsequent filer getting final approval.

When the innovator company files suit, a judge rather than a jury hears the case. It is typically resolved within the 30-month period by the patent being either held valid and infringed, or invalid or unenforceable due to some defect in the patent. If the patent is upheld, the Court will order the FDA not to finally approve the ANDA until the patent expires and all of the regulatory exclusivities, including the pediatric, have expired. Since the generic product is not on the market, there is no claim for damages allowed other than attempts to get attorneys' fees reimbursed. The Federal Circuit has ruled that the mere filing of an ANDA cannot be grounds for alleging willful infringement (*Glaxo v. Apotex* (Fed. Cir. 2004)) and such awards are seldom granted in the absence of particularly bad behavior by one of the parties.

If the patent is held invalid by the Federal District Court, the FDA is free to approve the generic product and the generic company is free to sell it. However, the innovator company may also appeal the decision of the lower court to the Court of Appeals for the Federal Circuit in Washington, DC, the only appeals court for patent cases. If that court reverses the lower court and upholds the patent, the generic company will be subject to damages for infringement if it has placed the generic product on the market.

This puts a big risk on the generic company to decide whether to sell "at risk" during the period of the appeal. Generic companies used to wait until the appeal decision had been handed down to avoid that risk, though lately they have become more aggressive and may launch the generic product after a favorable lower court ruling if they believe the decision will be affirmed. Despite the new rule providing that the 180-day exclusivity does not start until a decision by the Federal Circuit, some first-filers just can't wait for that decision before selling the generic product.

A few large generic companies like Teva, based in Israel, and Apotex, based in Canada, have made it clear by their actions that they will launch a generic at risk. Teva in particular accounts for the lion's share of at-risk launches in the U.S. However, this is a high stakes game and judgments or settlements resulting from at-risk launches where the patent was ultimately upheld can cost generic companies huge damages for lost profits if the patent is ultimately held valid. For example, in 2013, Teva and Sun Pharmaceutical agreed to pay Pfizer and Takeda $2.1 billion in damages for Teva's and Sun's at-risk launch of a generic for the drug Protonx in 2008, where it was estimated Pfizer lost roughly $2.9 billion in sales before the patent was upheld.

MEDICARE ACT AMENDMENTS

As mentioned earlier, some amendments to the Hatch Waxman Act were signed into law in December, 2003 as the Medicare

Prescription Drug Improvement and Modernization Act (the "Medicare Act"). The Medicare Act provides a number of important new rights and limitations including the following:

- limits drug companies to a single 30-month stay

- significantly amends the rules about the 180-day exclusivity for the first-filer generic company

- provides a right to generic companies to bring a declaratory judgment of patent infringement if the brand company fails to bring suit after a Paragraph IV certification

- allows a generic filer to challenge the propriety of an Orange Book listing if, after providing a Paragraph IV certification, it was sued on a patent it did not think should have been listed in the Orange Book

- provides that agreements between generic companies (who have provided Paragraph IV certifications) and innovators relating to the manufacturing, marketing or sale of the drug in question or market exclusivity must be filed with the Department of Justice and the Federal Trade Commission (FTC)

To get additional 30-month stays, innovator companies had been listing additional patents in the Orange Book long after the reference drug was approved and *after* they had received Paragraph IV certifications. These so-called "late listed" patents sometimes covered off-label indications (uses of the drug which were not approved by FDA, but which doctors were commonly prescribing the drug for), metabolites or various crystal structures and hydrates of the drug, and other variations on the active drug such as novel characteristics of the drug product formulation.

Generic companies were therefore subject to multiple 30-month stays as the innovator company was entitled to a 30-month stay for each late-listed patent, since the generic company was required to provide a Paragraph IV certification for each one listed in the Orange Book whether or not the generic company thought the listing was proper. The new law was intended to provide a single 30-month period by restricting the 30-month stay only to patents that were listed in the Orange Book *prior* to the filing of the ANDA.

I mention the Medicare Act Amendments (MMA) separately because there may be a few ANDA cases still wending their way through the courts based on pre-MMA rules and the outcomes in those cases may not apply to ANDAs filed after December, 2003.

Changes to 180-Day Exclusivity under the MMA

The law before the Medicare Act had some flaws regarding the 180-day exclusivity for generic companies. Since the previous law awarded this important exclusivity to the first filer, generic company employees lined up outside the FDA days and even weeks before the first day an ANDA could be filed to try to be first to obtain first-filer status. To stop this practice, the FDA issued a guidance that it would consider all filers who filed a complete ANDA on the same day to be "first-filers". The Medicare Act made this law.

The previous law also applied separately to each listed patent and therefore a generic company who filed an ANDA after the first-filer, but who was the first to file a Paragraph IV certification against a different or "late listed" patent, was also entitled to the 180-day exclusivity. This led to confusion and even litigation between different generic companies to establish which one was entitled to the 180-day exclusivity and when it would start. The new law simplified this by applying the 180-day exclusivity on a *product rather than a patent* basis, so now there is only one 180-day exclusivity per drug product and that is granted to the generic company that is (or companies that are) the first-filer for the product.

The new law also affects agreements between generic companies and branded companies intended to restrict the transfer of the 180-day exclusivity. Now, the first "commercial marketing" that triggers the 180-day period is not restricted to the first sale of an ANDA product, but is also triggered by the sale of the innovator drug as an "authorized generic", e.g., in a supply agreement between a generic company and a branded company. See Chapter 8 for more on authorized generics and how they have significantly changed the landscape for generic companies.

The new law also settled an issue about which court decision triggered the start of the 180-day period. Previously, the FDA had taken the position it was a "final" ruling and that required a ruling from the Federal Circuit. A later case concluded that the language of the statute meant any ruling and so the trigger was the District Court decision. This created a big problem for the first-filer because the 180-day exclusivity would be over before the appeal was decided. The new law makes it clear the trigger is a final decision by the District Court if there is no appeal or by the Federal Circuit if it is appealed.

Agreements Between Innovators and Generic Companies

The new law also requires any agreements or "deals" between innovators and generic companies that have filed a Paragraph IV certification must be reported to the FTC and Department of Justice. This was an attempt to put some sunlight on the now-challenged past practices of some innovator and generic companies entering into settlements of Hatch Waxman patent litigation in which the innovator made payments to the generic company to settle the case (so-called "reverse payment" cases), leaving the innovator's product on the market with no immediate generic product competition.

The result of this legislation initially had the effect of making settlements of such litigation more difficult since any compromise in which a generic company received something of value in exchange for dropping even a questionable suit had the potential of being considered improper by the authorities if the generic company agreed to delay entry into the market for any substantial period.

The FTC continued to take strong actions to discourage "reverse payment" settlements by starting investigations and bringing suit where it believed unfair practices had taken place. One such suit was against Schering-Plough. In 1997, Schering-Plough and its potential generic competitors settled patent infringement litigation with terms that included payments by Schering to the generic company. However, part of the deal was that Schering was licensed by the generic company giving Schering access to certain new products. Also part of the deal was the generic company agreed to delay introduction of the generic products. The FTC characterized the deal as a "reverse payment" to delay introduction of generic products and viewed the licensing deal as a cover-up.

In 2003 the full Commission overruled its administrative law judge and found Schering to be in violation of federal antitrust laws. However a unanimous 2005 opinion of the U.S. Court of Appeals for the 11th Circuit found in favor of Schering and set aside the FTC ruling, holding that the FTC's view, that automatically invalidated any agreement in which a patent-holding pharmaceutical manufacturer settled an infringement case by negotiating the generic product's entry date, was wrong.

In a second case in the Second Circuit (*In re Tamoxifen Citrate Antitrust Litigation 2005*) which involved an acknowledged reverse payment, the Second Circuit Court of Appeals likewise upheld the right of pharmaceutical companies to make reverse payments to settle Hatch Waxman cases based on the "scope of the patent" test which looks at primarily whether the agreed-upon generic entry date is later than the expiration of the patent. Under this test according to critics, reverse payment settlements are virtually immune from to the antitrust laws.

Other circuits applying the "scope of the patent" test included the Federal Circuit and again the 11th Circuit in *FTC v. Actavis* (11th Cir. 2012) where the FTC had challenged a reverse payment settlement between Solvey and Actavis over a generic version of Solvey's AndroGel. The FTC had sued the parties in 2009 alleging that in a settlement agreement of 2006, Solvey had unlawfully agreed to pay Actavis $19–30 million annually until 2015 when Actavis would be permitted to market its generic product, 5 years before Solvey's patent expired.

However, *In re K-Dur Antitrust Litigation* (3rd Cir. 2012), the Court reached the opposite conclusion based on what it called the "quick look" test, concluding that:

> "*the finder of fact must treat any payment from a patent holder to a generic patent challenger who agrees to delay entry into the market as a prima facie evidence of an unreasonable restraint of trade, which could be rebutted by showing the payment (1) was for a purpose other than delayed entry or (2) offers some pro-competitive benefit*".

The Supreme Court took the 11th Circuit FTC case to resolve the circuit split. It decided in a close 5 to 3 decision in *FTC v. Actavus* (Supreme Court 2013) that "reverse payment" settlements of ANDA litigation should be analyzed according to the "rule of reason" applied in antitrust law. Thus the Court compromised between the two opposed positions urged by the parties: that such settlements were presumptively illegal under the antitrust laws (FTC and 3rd Circuit) or that they are virtually immune from antitrust scrutiny (2rd and 11th Circuit Courts).

A conservative dissent written by Chief Justice Roberts argued that patent rights should be seen as an exception to the antitrust laws and that a patentee should have the right to enforce its patents or settle its patent suits without regard to the anticompetitive nature of any settlement.

Similarly in Europe, the EU's antitrust regulator announced in June, 2013 that it would impose "significant fines" on several

European drug firms including Denmark's Lundbeck for "reverse payment" settlements. The European Commission, the EU's antitrust regulator, can fine a company up to 10% of its global revenue for breaching anti-competition laws. The EU competition authority has similar cases pending against Teva, J&J, the French company Servier and Novartis.

The result of these decisions is that antitrust implications must now be considered for any major patent litigation settlement in the U.S. and Europe. In addition, the decision opens the door for antitrust action against patentees willing to settle cases below the likely litigation costs of the accused infringers. A further problem with the Supreme Court decision is that it does not explain how the "rule of reason" is to apply in patent infringement settlements, leaving drug and generic companies in the dark as to how they are supposed to legally settle cases in future.

Declaratory Judgment Actions

A recent 2007 Supreme Court case (*MedImmune v. Genentech*) provided the generic industry with some additional ammunition against a brand company that decides not to sue under a patent listed in the Orange Book. The *MedImmune* case related to the issue of whether a licensee in good standing could sue for a declaratory judgment of invalidity of the patent it was licensed under without first breaching the license agreement. The Supreme Court reversed the Federal Circuit and said yes and thereby changed the rules on when a company could properly sue for a declaratory judgment of patent invalidity.

The new law also added a new right for generic companies to file a declaratory judgment (DJ) action against the innovator if the innovator does not sue the generic company for patent infringement within the 45-day period provided after the generic company files the Paragraph IV certification. The generic industry wanted this right in the event the innovators did *not* sue them in response to a Paragraph IV certification, because this put the generic industry at risk of suit when it obtained approval and manufactured and launched the product. The generic industry wanted the right to have the patent litigation resolved before the generic product was approved.

In order to file such a DJ action, a generic company must also provide confidential access to its ANDA so that the innovator can assess whether the generic product is infringing. No such confidential access is required if the Paragraph IV certification only relates to patent invalidity. In combination with the Supreme Court ruling in the *MedImmune* case discussed above, this legislation has been reasonably effective in allowing such suits to go forward in the courts.

Counterclaim to De-list

Finally the new law provides that a generic company can counterclaim to de-list a patent that it thinks should not have been listed in the Orange Book. This was intended to provide the generic industry with the right to challenge Orange Book listings as previous court decisions indicated they could not be challenged and the generic industry thought that encouraged listing of frivolous patents. This new right is limited as it cannot be brought independently (only as a counter-claim to a suit by the innovator) and the only remedy allowed is de-listing of the improperly listed patent, i.e., no money damages allowed.

Patent Challenges on the Increase

A research company (Stanford group) reported in 2010 that patent challenges continue to increase with 51 new first-to-file lawsuits filed in 2008, up from 13 in 2003. Based on a review of 270 rulings over 8 years, the report concluded that of the cases that go to trial, the overall success rate in patent challenges is about even with generics winning 25% of the time and brands winning 27% of the time, and with a majority of the cases (42%) being settled. And when a generic wins, it will most likely be upheld on appeal as only 2 of 92 cases were overturned against the generic.

The three top courts by case volume were New Jersey, Delaware and the Southern District of New York, which collectively accounted for almost 70% of all decisions. Not surprisingly, because the brand company selects the venue for the suit, those three districts were pro-brand (70% of the time). Pro-generic courts included the Central District of California. Settlements have also increased following the June, 2006 decision by the U.S. Supreme Court declining to hear the FTC's appeal in the *Schering* case regarding reverse payments, but will no doubt decrease now that the Supreme Court ruled in 2013 that the antitrust "rule of reason" applies to such patent infringement settlements.

CANADA

In General

The only other country to have a similar statute as Hatch Waxman is Canada. In Canada the innovator company is similarly allowed to list its patents covering its approved drug products in a government registry and ANDA filers in Canada must likewise provide notice to innovator companies if they intend to challenge the listed patents. Innovator companies can likewise file suit for infringement within a defined period and if they do, the Canadian health authorities may not approve the ANDA for two years, unless a court decides the patent is invalid before the two-year period is up.

Paragraph IV Letters

A curious aspect of this procedure in Canada is that while the law in Canada requires a generic company to send the equivalent

Paragraph IV certification, it does not have to be truthful, based on a Canadian Court of Appeals decision (*Syntex and Allergan v. Apotex* 2003) which the Canadian Supreme Court chose not to review. Thus the generic company may legally hide the fact that it is infringing a patent by, for example, making ambiguous statements about the formulation of its product. If the innovator fails to sue for infringement within the time provided, the innovator company has no right to sue under the statute after the time for suit had passed and that any alleged fraud or misrepresentation must be addressed in a separate suit for patent infringement after the generic product has been approved and launched. This also allows the generic company to launch the generic drug when it is approved and the only thing the brand company can do is sue for damages since Canadian Courts rarely, if ever, grant preliminary injunctions in patent cases.

This places every innovator with products in Canada in the odd position of having to sue every generic company that sends a notice letter if it wants to be sure to get the two year hold on approval for the generic while it litigates the case. This is an example of how Canadian governmental policy and even the Canadian Courts favor generics over innovators. And since the average patent case in Canada takes about four years to get to trial, the two-year holding period is totally inadequate and results in the product being genericized most of the time. The net result is that trying to prevent generics with patents in Canada is an expensive, frustrating and generally unrewarding activity.

Listing Requirements

Canada also has the same requirement that patents must be listed within 30 days of grant with the health authorities in Canada. However, in Canada this is set in stone, and if the innovator company misses this date by even one day, the right to receive the ANDA filing notice from the generic company is lost. This is a real burden on the innovator company to accomplish consistently, since it has to have close coordination between its Canadian patent agents and its U.S. internal patent and regulatory departments in order to get this done within the short time permitted. This is especially the case where an important patent is licensed from a third party whose Canadian patent agents may not be aware of the urgency involved and may take some time to report the new grant to the licensor who then must report it to the drug holder in time to make the filing. The U.S. has a similar 30-day filing rule, but there is no penalty or loss of rights in the U.S. for late filing as long as the patent is listed before a generic company files its ANDA, a sort of "no harm, no foul" rule.

Prior to the new regulations, there was no restriction in Canada to filing additional patents after the generic company had sent its first patent notification to the innovator. If an additional patent was listed, the generic company was required to send another notification and the innovator was entitled to sue again and got another two years in which the Canadian FDA could not approve the generic drug. Effective June 17, 2006, this is no longer the law and one can no longer list a patent on the patent register for an innovative drug after a generic submission has been made for the drug. Likewise, in order to be listed, the patent must contain a claim for the medicine itself, its approved use or a formulation or dosage form covering the approved product. Patents without direct therapeutic application, such as processes or intermediates may not be listed, nor may off-label patents be listed.

Canada also has another "catch". In order to list a patent in Canada, the brand company must have filed the patent application *in Canada* or filed a PCT application naming Canada *prior to filing its drug dossier* as a New Drug Submission (NDS) with the Canadian FDA. One way around this is to file a Supplemental New Drug Submission (SNDS) for a change in dosage form or new use of the drug and then the patent may be listed prior to the SNDS filing if it contains a claim for the new dosage form or new use.

In 2013, frustrated with how its patents have been treated in Canada, Eli Lilly filed a $500 million dollar NAFTA suit against Canada. The NAFTA claim alleges that several Canadian court rulings invalidating the patents for its drugs Straterra and Zyprexa were illegal under international law because they violated Canada's obligations under Chapter 11 of NAFTA, the international trade treaty that covers the U.S., Canada and Mexico.

Chapter 11 protects the investments of companies and investors from NAFTA countries that operate in other NAFTA states. Eli Lilly alleges Canada violated the provisions of Chapter 11 that guarantee fair and equal treatment to foreign investors and protects them from expropriation of their investments. A spokesman for Lilly was quoted as saying "Patent decisions in Canada over the last decade not only fly in the face of long-established international standards, but they're subjective and completely unpredictable".

Exclusivity

The eight-year exclusivity (six years of data exclusivity plus two years of marketing exclusivity) provided by the new regulations applies only for new chemical entities (NCEs) approved after June 17, 2006 that were not previously approved in Canada. Excluded from obtaining this exclusivity are variations of a previously approved drug such as salts, esters, polymorphs, etc. Likewise, new uses of old drugs and combinations of old drugs are not considered new drugs and do not get any exclusivity in Canada. In contrast, under EU law, novel combinations of old drugs are treated as new drugs for purposes of being eligible for regulatory exclusivity and patent term extensions. In the U.S. such combinations are considered old drugs, but are eligible for the three-year exclusivity for new formulations or new uses, but are not eligible for patent term extensions.

An exception to the six-year data exclusivity is that a generic company may file an application for authorization to export a drug to a third world country under a special law allowing for that. However, approval to sell in Canada may not be given until the end of the eight-year period.

The new regulations also provide for a six-month pediatric exclusivity that is added to the eight-year NCE exclusivity. However, in contrast to the U.S. pediatric exclusivity, the six months is not also added to the effective patent life for the drug. In order to be eligible, pediatric clinical studies must be submitted within five years of the NCE approval.

Patented Medicine Prices Review Board

Canada also has the Patented Medicine Prices Review Board (PMPRB). It is intended to protect consumers in Canada by ensuring that prices charged for patented drugs are not excessive. As a result, all patents that pertain to a patented medicine must be listed with the PMPRB. Non-compliance can result in fines, payback of excessive pricing and even jail time. The PMPRB looks at pricing of the same drug in a number of countries around the world and sets a maximum price around the average.

A curious incongruity of the PMPRB rules and the new drug exclusivity rules is that only certain drug-related patents may be listed for purposes of obtaining and maintaining exclusivity, but all drug-related patents must be submitted to the PMPRB and that submission gives the PMPRB authority to set maximum prices for the drug. Therefore, if one has a potential for obtaining a patent in Canada that is the wrong type of patent to be listable, and therefore not that useful in obtaining or maintaining exclusivity, one might think about *not* filing the patent in Canada so that the drug would not be subject to price controls.

I'm told by Canadian lawyers that the PMPRB has also recently started looking into the fact that generic companies are also filing patents for some of their generic products and the PMPRB takes the position that that makes the generics subject to their jurisdiction. The generics reply that that is ridiculous, but we shall have to wait and see how that turns out, bearing in mind generic product prices are higher in Canada than in the U.S.

TAKE HOME MESSAGE

• The Hatch Waxman Act provides generic companies the right to copy innovator's drugs after certain defined exclusivity periods have elapsed and provides innovators patent term extensions of up to five years to make up for some of the time lost in obtaining approval to market from FDA.

• Therapeutic equivalence (TE) requires an FDA determination that a generic drug product is both pharmaceutically equivalent (same active ingredient(s), dosage form, strength or concentration and same route of administration) and bioequivalent (acts the same in the body) to the branded drug product.

• A generic drug with an A rating such as AB or AT is considered therapeutically equivalent to the corresponding brand drug and can be freely substituted for a brand drug at the pharmacy level without permission of the doctor. A generic drug with a B rating cannot be substituted at the pharmacy level without the doctor's specific approval.

• Patents are listed in the Orange Book by brand companies with use codes for method of use patents.

• A generic company must make a patent certification to any Orange Book listing as part of an ANDA or 505(b)(2) filing.

• A Paragraph I or II certification means the FDA may approve the ANDA when it is ready.

• A Paragraph III certification means the FDA will approve the ANDA when the last listed patent in the Orange Book expires.

- A Paragraph IV certification means that the generic company is either alleging non-infringement of all listed patents or challenging the validity of one or more of the listed patents in the Orange Book.

- An innovator has 45 days from receipt of a Paragraph IV certification to sue the generic company for infringement.

- If suit is filed, the FDA is barred from approving the ANDA for 30 months, or for any such shorter period if a District Court rules on the patent challenge in less than 30 months.

- Medicare Act Amendments allow only one 30-month period for each ANDA or 505(b)(2) filed and off-label use patents may not be listed in the Orange Book.

- Patent infringement settlement agreements between generic companies and innovators must be reported to the Justice Department and FTC. "Reverse payments" settlement agreements are subject to the antitrust "rule of reason".

- Canada has a similar statutory scheme and bars the health authorities from approving a generic drug for two years from the patent certification date.

The next Chapter discusses **Generics for Biological Drugs** or so-called "biosimilars" which technically are not covered by the Hatch Waxman Act, but are covered in new legislation passed in 2010 amending the Public Health Safety Act.

Chapter 7

Generics for Biological Drugs

INTRODUCTION

The field of biogenerics, or so-called "biosimilars", as the FDA now refers to them, will be a reality very soon. Previously the FDA hinted that the first likely biological products it would consider for generic approvals were the older drugs, recombinant human insulin and human growth hormone. Historically, these drugs were approved as NDAs, making them technically more subject to becoming generic drugs than other biotech drugs that were approved under a different legal scheme and were filed as Biological License Applications (BLAs). This is because historically, BLAs were for biologically derived medicines and products and were under the jurisdiction of a different branch of FDA than the branch responsible for drugs. Recently FDA has transferred some functions of CBER (the biologicals division) to CDER (the drug division) to provide more uniformity for drug and biologic evaluations.

Story of Erythropoietin (EPO)

Biologics are typically large protein molecules derived from living material including human, animal or microorganism. They

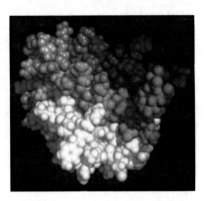

8. Molecular structure of Erythropoietin

are complex in structure and often are not fully characterized. An example of arguably the most important biological since insulin is erythropoietin or EPO.

Researchers had long speculated that there was a natural substance or hormone in the blood that stimulated the production of red blood cells, but it existed in such small quantities it could not be isolated. In 1955, a young biochemist by the name of Eugene Goldwasser decided to try. After 20 years of effort at the University of Chicago, he was finally successful.

An important breakthrough came when he discovered EPO could be found in the kidneys, which explained why people with chronic kidney disease became anemic. By 1971, he was still only able to purify EPO in small microgram quantities from anemic sheep. A few years later, on the suggestion of a Japanese colleague, Dr. Takaji Miyake, that EPO might be found in patients suffering from aplastic anemia, he was finally able to obtain isolated human EPO in milligram quantities from a concentrate of 675 gallons of urine from such patients.

That allowed him to provide a small amount of EPO to Amgen in 1975, where a geneticist cloned the gene for EPO, and by inserting the gene into hamster cells using recently developed biotech techniques, Amgen was ultimately able to manufacture EPO in sufficient quantities for use as the blockbuster drug Epogen, which was approved by FDA in 1989. EPO stimulates the production of red blood cells and corrects the anemia of dialysis patients and other anemia sufferers and has saved or improved the lives of millions of people around the world. Under the "compound in a bottle" test, EPO would have been patentable even though it was a naturally occurring substance. This is a good example of why denying patentability merely because a substance is naturally occurring is not good public policy in my opinion. The fact that EPO existed naturally did not help millions of anemia sufferers and the patent system is designed to encourage discoveries of the type made by Goldwasser for the betterment of mankind. As a historical footnote, Goldwasser in fact did not file a patent on his meritorious practical discovery and isolation of EPO, though of course Amgen filed many thereafter.

EARLY APPROVALS OF BIOLOGICAL GENERICS

Swiss Sandoz's Omnitrope (somatropin), a copy of a recombinant human growth hormone, was approved in Australia in 2004. In 2006, the European Commission approved Omnitrope as the first authorization of a "similar biological medicinal product" or "biosimilar" under EU pharmaceutical marketing authorization legislation. Omnitrope was also approved thereafter by the FDA in 2006, but not as a biosimilar or biogeneric or follow-on biologic. Instead, Sandoz filed the drug as a 505(b)(2) filing (so-called paper NDA) to become the first copy of a recombinant biotechnology drug to be approved in the U.S. in this manner.

However, the FDA stated on its website that its approval of Omnitrope for children with growth disorders "does not establish a pathway for approval" for generic biologics and said Congress needed to pass legislation to give the agency such authority. FDA approval followed a successful lawsuit by Sandoz demanding that

FDA take action on its submission. U.S. legislation for generic biologics which had been pending since 2007 was finally approved in 2010.

U.S. LAW FOR BIOSIMILARS

The Patient Protection and Affordable Care Act was signed into law by President Obama on March 23, 2010. This new law amends the Public Health Service Act (PHS Act) and for the first time creates an abbreviated approval pathway for biological products that are demonstrated to be "highly similar" (biosimilar) to or "interchangeable" with an FDA-approved biological product. FDA says it will refer to these new statutory provisions as the Biologics Price Competition and Innovation Act of 2009 (BPCI Act).

The new legislation establishes two different categories of biological products approvable under the abbreviated pathway: biological products that are "biosimilar" to an approved biological product and biological products that are "interchangeable" with an approved biological product.

FDA says that under the BPCI Act, a sponsor may seek approval of a biosimilar product under new section 351(k) of the PHS Act if it submits data showing that the product is "highly similar" to the reference biological product, notwithstanding minor differences in clinically inactive components, and there are no clinically meaningful differences between the biosimilar product and the reference product in terms of safety, purity and potency.

FDA further says that in order to meet the higher standard of "interchangeability", a sponsor must demonstrate that the biosimilar product can be expected to produce the same clinical result as the reference product in any given patient and, for a biological product that is administered more than once, that the risk of alternating or switching between the biosimilar product and the reference product is not greater than the risk of maintaining the patient on the reference product.

Only interchangeable biosimilars are eligible for market exclusivity and that exclusivity is only with respect to other interchangeable biosimilars. That is, if FDA approves a biosimilar as "interchangeable", it will not approve another interchangeable biosimilar for that reference product during the exclusivity period, though there are no such restrictions on approval of another biosimilar of that reference product.

The exclusivity period for the first interchangeable biosimilar is between 12 and 42 months depending on the circumstances and is for the earlier of 12 months from marketing, 18 months from a final court decision of patent litigation or 18 months from approval if there has been no patent litigation and 42 months if the patent litigation is still ongoing.

Interchangeable biosimilars are considered therapeutically equivalent to the brand biological reference product and therefore may be substituted at the pharmacy for the brand product, as is the case for an "A" rated generic drug. Biosimilars are like "B" rated generic drugs and are not considered therapeutically equivalent to the branded biological product and are not allowed to be substituted at the pharmacy for the brand product without authorization by a physician.

Finally, biosimilars are deemed to contain a new active ingredient while interchangeables are considered to contain the same active as the brand product. That fact will further deter physicians from authorizing substitution of a biosimilar for an approved biological drug, since they are not even considered to contain the same drug compound.

In order to obtain FDA approval, an applicant must demonstrate that the biological product is biosimilar to the reference product based on analytical studies, animal studies and clinical studies, that it uses the same mechanism of action, the same route of administration, dosage form and strength and is for the same indication or use. In addition, the facility in which the biosimilar will be manufactured has to meet current standards for safety, purity and potency. The legislation also provides the FDA with the discretion to waive any of the foregoing requirements.

Branded biological products approved as BLAs are entitled up to 12.5 years of exclusivity from date of approval, consisting of 4 years of data exclusivity, 8 years of marketing exclusivity and 6 months of pediatric exclusivity. That means applications for approval of a biosimilar for such a reference product will not be accepted by FDA until 4 years after approval and no biosimilar may be approved until the end of 12 or 12.5 years from approval of the reference product. No exclusivity is provided for new supplements, new indications or routes of administration, new dosing schedules, new dosage forms, new delivery systems or devices, or new strengths, or modifications that do not result in changes in safety, purity or potency.

This new 12 year exclusivity for biological products is far longer than the 5 year NCE exclusivity provided for new conventional drugs under the Hatch Waxman rules and will likely have a profound effect on the future commercial thinking of the pharma industry. A number of large pharma companies around the world have already reported that they are planning to focus future R&D investment on obtaining approval of new biological products.

There is a patent dispute procedure which is brand friendly and frankly too complicated to go into any detail, and leaves many unanswered questions because it assumes the parties can work out between themselves which patents should be litigated and when. There is no 30 month stay and no Orange Book listing and no exclusivity for challenging a patent. The legislation also requires that the biosimilar applicant provide the brand company with all of its proprietary manufacturing methodology for non-infringement claims, and 6 months prior notice of its intent to enter the commercial market, which would provide the brand company an opportunity to seek a preliminary injunction to prevent launch of the biosimilar if there were pending patent infringement litigation.

The reason the biosimilar statute is so favourable to the brand industry and not more favourable to the generic industry is that it was a brand industry written bill that was simply appended to the "Obamacare" bill which was then passed by Congress without the opportunity for amendment. As a result, biosimilars did not get a very good foundation at birth.

In 2012, the FDA finally announced publication of three "draft" guidance documents on biosimilar product development to assist industry in developing such products in the U.S. The three guidance documents relate to "Scientific" and "Quality" considerations in demonstrating biosimilarity to a referenced product and a Q and A regarding the 2009 statute. It is not known if or when the draft guidance will become final. Here is what the FDA says about them:

Scientific Considerations in Demonstrating Biosimilarity to a Reference Product: The draft guidance is intended to assist companies in demonstrating that a proposed therapeutic protein product is biosimilar to a reference product for the purpose of submitting an application, called a "351(k)" application, to the FDA. This draft guidance describes a risk-based "totality-of-the-evidence" approach that the FDA intends to use to evaluate the data and information submitted in support of a determination of biosimilarity of the proposed product to the reference product. As outlined in the draft guidance, FDA recommends a stepwise approach in the development of biosimilar products.

Quality Considerations in Demonstrating Biosimilarity to a Reference Protein Product: The draft guidance provides an overview of analytical factors to consider when assessing biosimilarity between a proposed therapeutic protein product and a reference product for the purpose of submitting a 351(k) application. This includes the importance of extensive analytical, physico-chemical and biological characterization in demonstrating that the proposed biosimilar product is highly similar to the reference product notwithstanding minor differences in clinically inactive components.

Biosimilars: Questions and Answers Regarding Implementation of the Biologics Price Competition and Innovation Act of 2009: The draft guidance provides answers to common questions from people interested in developing biosimilar products. The question and answer format addresses questions that may arise in the early stages of product development, such as how to request meetings with the FDA, addressing differences in formulation from the reference product, how to request exclusivity, and other topics.

Notwithstanding the foregoing advice from FDA, companies continue to face delays and obstacles in copying biotech drugs for the U.S. market. Reasons for the delays include the technical difficulties of replicating such complex molecules and patent protections, as well as unclear rules on what is required for approval. And branded companies are also seeking to delay biosimilar competition to their top selling products by fortifying patents and lobbying state legislators to make it more difficult to substitute a biosimilar for its corresponding branded product.

Merck's decision to end efforts to copy one of Amgen's blockbuster drug shows how the emerging field of developing generic versions of biotechnology medicines won't be easy to enter. Development of biosimilars is expected to be costly and complex, especially if FDA requires extensive clinical studies, which FDA requested in Merck's case and was one reason Merck gave for not completing development. Merck says it remains committed to biosimilars by investing more than $1.5 billion by 2015.

Recently, Novartis highlighted the advancement of its biosimilar pipeline, noting its Sandoz unit is running seven phase III studies across five biosimilar molecules including a phase III study in the U.S. for a biosimilar version of Epogen (EPO); and Pfizer reported carrying out several phase I and II studies in biosimilars.

In sizing up the opportunity, Teva projected that about $53 billion in branded biologic sales will be exposed to biosimilar competition by 2015 through patent expirations alone. Analysts believe biosimilars will likely have their own brands and will not be automatically substitutable, which means they will not experience the immediate market gains seen with traditional generics that take majority market share in a matter of months.

European Regulations for Biosimilars

Europe remains well ahead of the U.S. with regard to biosimilar regulatory matters. The EMA had already approved 13 biosimilars as of 2010, including generic versions of human growth hormone, erythropoietin (EPO) and G-CSF. In late 2010, the EMA published guidelines for biosimilar antibodies. In 2013, the EMA said its experts backed approval of a biosimilar version of J&J's blockbuster antibody-based rheumatoid arthritis drug Remicade. Antibodies represent a substantial economic opportunity for generic manufacturers both in the U.S. and Europe and generic companies are eager to enter the multibillion-dollar antibody market as the patents on key brand products expire.

Pricing of biosimilars has also affected the market for biological products in Europe. For example, France's compulsory price discounts for generic drugs have been applied to EPO and somatropin biosimilars and mandated price reductions for the brand versions have made prices roughly equivalent. In Germany three biosimilars entered the market at 30% below the originator price. Price reductions by the originator were followed by further price reductions by the biosimilars. The result is that biosimilars will eventually bring down the cost of biological products and in doing so will likely expand the market.

As mentioned earlier, drug giant Sandoz, the generic business unit of Novartis, is a pioneer and global leader in this field. Sandoz introduced the first biosimilar (human growth hormone somatropin) between 2006 and 2009 in Europe, North America and Japan. Sandoz' biosimilars had total global sales of $261 million in 2011, less than 2% of global sales levels for branded biologicals of $157 billion in 2011, suggesting future commercial opportunities for biosimilars have just begun.

Biosimilars in India

Major Indian drug manufacturers such as Dr. Reddy, Sun Pharma and Ranbaxy are already major suppliers of generic drugs in India and around the world, including the U.S. Now they are into biosimilars. India is a semi-regulated market and requires only modest phase III studies for biosimilars. As a result, there are a number of such biosimilars being sold in India including copies of Amgen's Neupogen, Aranesp and Neulasta and Roche's Rituxan.

TAKE HOME MESSAGE

- U.S. legislation authorizing generic versions of biological products in the form of "biosimilars" was passed into law on March 23, 2010.

- For branded biological products, the new law provides up to 12.5 years of exclusivity consisting of 4 years data exclusivity, 8 years marketing exclusivity and 6 months pediatric exclusivity.

- For approved biological generics ("biosimilars"), the new law provides 12–42 months exclusivity for approved biosimilars which are determined to be "interchangeable" and therefore substitutable at the pharmacy for the reference biological product.

- Biosimilars that are not found to be interchangeable are not substitutable at the pharmacy and receive no exclusivity.

- There is no Orange Book listing, no 30 month litigation stay and no exclusivity granted for challenging a patent.

- Patent dispute procedures are provided, but are complicated and not very workable.

The next Chapter discusses how to use the information previously developed on patents, FDA, regulatory exclusivity and the Hatch Waxman Act to bring about **Product Life-Cycle Management.**

Chapter 8

Putting it All Together: Product Life-Cycle Management

Brand name drug owners have developed strategies to protect their long-term investments and current sales despite the right of generic companies to copy innovators and obtain approvals of generic drugs in the absence of patent protection after the limited exclusivity periods described in previous chapters have expired. These strategies are known generally as product life-cycle management and are intended to extend the life of innovator products. Professionals involved in strategic marketing also have developed a number of non-product-oriented techniques to enhance a product's success, but the focus of this chapter will be on product life-cycle management by use of patents, regulatory strategies, product improvements and the Hatch Waxman Act.

The FTC has another view of pharmaceutical product life-cycle management and refers to it as "product hopping" or "evergreening", which an FTC commissioner described as the practice of

> "introducing new patented products with minor or no substantive improvements in the hopes of preventing substitution to lower priced generics."

As of late 2013, there is no case law that supports the FTC in any meaningful way, though antitrust claims under the Sherman Act have been brought by generic companies in a few lower court cases, one with support from the FTC. In obtaining leave to file an amicus brief in *Mylan v. Warner Chilcott* (E.D. Pa. 2012), the FTC said that *"…pharmaceutical product redesigns can constitute exclusionary conduct."*

In reply, Warner says that only three courts have even considered claims that new pharmaceutical products constitute illegal switching in violation of the antitrust laws. Two of them dismissed those claims, while one allowed the case to proceed, but that case was settled before judgment. So at this point in time (late 2013), LCM is still alive and kicking, despite the FTC.

Generally, life-cycle management (LCM) starts early and ideally is integrated into the entire development cycle itself. That is, even before the product has been developed, the people responsible for development and marketing must have in mind the need to provide an adequate life to the product. LCM involves a number of interactive strategies designed to enhance product life through the primary forms of exclusivity available to pharmaceutical products, through an interactive mix of a variety of techniques including patents, product improvements, FDA exclusivity, FDA Citizen Petitions and litigation, all at different stages in the product life cycle.

PATENTS

A product life cycle begins in the initial discovery of a promising lead compound. The first patents are intended to cover the general chemical family or genus of compounds; so patent claims are directed broadly to cover the genus as well as narrowly to cover the lead compound and variations in between. The main emphasis is on the chemical side—identifying chemical structures and methods of manufacturing them.

Development Stage

During the development stage where the pre-clinical, pharmacological and other biological aspects of the lead compound are evaluated, additional patents can be filed on newly discovered medical uses and novel formulations for the drug to enhance efficacy or to overcome drug metabolism or drug delivery issues. Improved methods of manufacture may be developed at that time for scale-up in preparation for clinical trials.

Clinical Stage

During the clinical stage, where the drug is tested in humans, additional patents can be filed on new dosage forms, methods of administration, potential new uses which may come to the attention of clinicians as side effects (which was how Viagra was discovered) and possible novel drug combinations with other known drugs. Pharmacokinetic data can also reveal patentable aspects of drugs, e.g., a pH change in an ophthalmic solution can unexpectedly enhance drug absorption through the cornea allowing a lower concentration of active drug resulting in reduced side effects. During this period, additional drug forms also may be identified, such as active metabolites or stereoisomers of the drug having unique characteristics, and polymorphs of the drug such as different crystal structures or hydrates (combinations of the solid drug with water).

Line Extensions, New Uses and Formulations

While the drug is pending approval, there is time to think about line extensions, potential new medical uses, improved formulations for better drug delivery, such as sustained release formulations or once-a-day administration, and improvements in the bulk synthesis of the active drug. Once approved and sold, shortcomings of the drug formulation relating to patient acceptance may come to light that were not apparent from the clinical trials. At this point, an improved formulation may be started to overcome the shortcoming. In addition, work may start on a single isomer improvement or drug combinations with other active drugs.

These techniques typically are applied to innovator drugs, but the same concept applies to a paper NDA drug filing under 505(b)(2) which involves some minor change in the innovator drug or its formulation that may be patentable itself. An example of this is Alcon modifying a patented formulation of an improvement of an innovator ophthalmic drug sold by Merck (Timolol XE) by using a different gelling agent to get around Merck's patent on its once-a-day drug formulation and at the same time patenting its own new formulation to prevent generics copying its new product.

Patent Term Adjustments and Extensions

Any patent term adjustment or extension that is available for the product should be sought worldwide. Typical extensions of up to five years are obtainable in the U.S. as well as Europe, Japan, Australia and other countries. The rules in each country vary, but each country provides formulas to make up for some, but not all of the patent time lost while the drug is going through the required regulatory approval hurdles.

The U.S. Patent Office (PTO) also provides a patent term *adjustment* to make up for certain delays in prosecution caused by the PTO. The rules are very tricky and the PTO often makes mistakes, which has generated a cottage industry to double check the PTO's determination of patent term adjustment. Patent prosecutors must also be aware of these rules since delays by the applicant offset delays by the PTO. For a billion dollar drug, even the loss of only one week's sales can be worth tens of millions of dollars. So when your outside counsel says he is too busy to work on your case and needs a 3-month extension at the PTO, tell him to get to work since that delay could ultimately reduce sales of your drug by $250 million!

In the U.S. the formula for patent term extension adds a maximum extension of five years to the original patent life, but not longer than 14 years of patent life from date of approval of the drug. The actual term is computed by a formula that applies to the period between IND filing and FDA approval of the NDA. The formula basically provides a day for every day the FDA is working on the file and a half-day for every day the applicant is working on the file. Typical patent term extensions are in the range of two to four years. The Patent Office confirms the dates submitted by the patent holder with the FDA and awards the patent term extension after publication in the Federal Register for complaints by interested parties.

The patent term extension does not actually extend the term of a patent for all of its claims. The patent term is extended only for the approved drug product. The question arises then what *exactly* is the approved drug product?

In an interesting case (*Pfizer v. Dr. Reddy*, Fed. Cir. 2004), a generic company, Dr. Reddy, took the position against the innovator, Pfizer, that a different ester of an active drug was not covered by the patent term extension and got a Federal District Court to agree. The industry was up in arms over this because such a ruling would make a mockery of the concept of patent term extension if insignificant changes in the approved drug product would not be covered by the patent term extension. In this case, it did not matter which ester was used for the drug, as the active drug moiety was the same regardless which ester was used. The Court of Appeals overruled the lower court, finding that the "approved drug product" meant the active drug moiety and not the exact chemical form of the approved drug.

The result of this case makes it clear that generic companies will not be able to make slight changes in salts or esters or hydrates of an active drug to get around a patent term extension. In addition improvements by the innovator, which incorporate the same active drug moiety, and which were approved drugs at the time the patent term extension was granted, are also entitled to protection under the original patent term extension and therefore encourage such improvements.

PRODUCT IMPROVEMENTS

The heart of LCM is product improvements following the launch of an original new chemical entity (NCE). These product improvements enable the innovator to improve the product at minimal cost compared to developing an entirely new NCE, while at the same time dramatically enhancing the future value of the NCE by providing improved medicines to the public and thereby extending its useful life.

Active Drug Combinations

Suitable improvements fall into a number of well-known categories including new excipients that may be used alone or in combination with new dosage forms or concentrations of the NCE to reduce side effects and/or to enhance patient comfort or compliance. Line extensions, such as combinations of different active drugs, for example, in the ophthalmic industry, where drugs are used in combination such as topical steroids combined with antibiotics to treat infection and inflammation.

An example of combining two known drugs for patient benefit is Vytorin, a combination approved by FDA in 2004. Vytorin is a combination of two well-known cholesterol-lowering drugs: Merck's Zocor and Schering-Plough's Zetia. The patent for Zocor expired in 2006 so the combination with the longer basic patent life of Zetia (2013) made good business sense as well as medical sense, since Zetia limits absorption of cholesterol in the digestive tract while Zocor, a statin, limits cholesterol production in the liver. The combination reduces cholesterol about an extra 20%.

Single Isomers

If the original drug was a racemate (an NCE consisting of two optical isomers—think of it as equal amounts of a left-handed and a right-handed version of the same chemical compound), a typical improvement is use of one of the isomers alone that sometimes has better biological activity or lesser or fewer side effects relative to the other isomer and the racemate. An example of this is the prescription successor to Prilosec, named Nexium, and promoted as the "Purple Pill", by Astra Zeneca. However, this strategy is no longer at the top of the LCM list for a number of reasons.

One potential problem with developing single isomers from known racemates is their potential for limited exclusivity, with one exception. The FDA generally considers them new formulations rather than new chemical entities (NCEs) so that the FDA exclusivity is only three years rather than the five years for an NCE. The exception under recent legislation is that a single isomer is entitled to the five-year exclusivity if it goes through an independent approval cycle and is not labelled for any use of the approved racemic for 10 years from approval.

On the negative side, recent cases have held some stereoisomer patents invalid on the grounds of obviousness. For example, the European patent for Nexium was held invalid, as was the U.S. patent for Altace. However, the U.S. patent for Lexapro was recently upheld. As the law now stands, if the stereoisomer has unexpected properties not found in the racemate and/or if it is not obvious how to separate the stereoisomer from the racemate, the stereoisomer may be patentable. Also on the positive side, recent cases have found patents for single isomers to be eligible for patent term extension even if the patent for the racemic was previously extended.

New Dosage Forms, Delivery Systems and Conditions of Use

Examples of new dosage forms are capsule to tablet and immediate release to extended release. One could also consider new strengths with improved bioavailability, active metabolites, polymorphs or new salts. New delivery systems, such as transdermal patches instead of oral delivery, and controlled release formulations for oral delivery, provide once-a-day dosing versus multiple-times-a-day dosing. Patients find this more convenient and doctors prefer it for improved patient compliance, i.e., the patient will more likely take the proper dose of the drug.

New and possibly patented conditions of use, such as new dosing or new indications, or safety regimens, combined with proper labelling, can be used to discourage a Section 8 "carve-out" where the generic requests that the FDA omit the Orange Book-listed patented use from the label. Such a carve-out is not permitted if to do so would render the generic less safe for the remaining labelled uses.

Another approach could be if the same drug formulation originally dosed twice-a-day was found to be just as effective with a once-a-day treatment, as in the case of two glaucoma products Xibrom (bromfenac) 0.09% and Bromday (bromfenac) 0.09%. Though the formulations were identical, the new once-a-day label change entitled Bromday, the once-a-day labelled product, to a new three-year exclusivity term based on the change in the label instructions for Xibrom which provide a new condition of use.

Each of the foregoing product improvements is entitled to a three-year FDA exclusivity if clinical trials were required for FDA approval, and of course it is likely that the new formulation, combination, condition of use or delivery system may be patentable. If the improvement provides valuable new benefits, doctors will prescribe the new formulation instead of the old one, and so a generic company will not be able to make much headway in trying to sell the older, less convenient or more difficult-to-use version of the drug.

Even without a patent, the additional three-year exclusivity would extend the life of a product significantly, since typical product life is only about 12–14 years even if the product is patented. (Recall one cannot even get a patent term extension if there is more than 14 years of life remaining on a patent.) And one can provide a series of such improvements such that successive three year exclusivities can greatly enhance the total product portfolio. For an example of this strategy, see the Alphagan example later in this chapter.

Orange Book Listing and De-listing

There is a further interactive effect with FDA and patents on improvements. If the innovator gets a patent on the improvement, the patent must be listed in the Orange Book. If a generic company wants to copy the improvement after the three-year exclusivity, it must file another ANDA and another Paragraph IV certification and the innovator can sue again under the Hatch Waxman Act and the FDA is prevented from granting an ANDA on the improvement for another 30 months.

Regarding de-listing of a patent in the Orange Book, while a generic company may challenge a patent listing in the Orange Book in a Hatch Waxman case by filing a counterclaim seeking a de-listing order, FDA generally defers to the NDA holder on whether to de-list. However, FDA may delay or refuse de-listing a patent if there has been Hatch Waxman litigation and de-listing could forfeit a first-filer's 180-day exclusivity; and current case law holds that the courts will not allow a patent holder to unilaterally deprive a generic of its 180-day exclusivity by delisting an Orange Book patent after the Paragraph IV certification has been provided.

Original Product Replacement

Another strategy is to launch the improvement early enough so that the innovator can inform patients and doctors about the improvement and if doctors and patients switch to the improvement, the original product may lose much of its market before a generic drug is approved. When the generic drug is approved, there is essentially no market for it since all the patients are using the improvement instead. In some cases, e.g., if the improvement relates to improved safety, the original product can be withdrawn from the market making it even more difficult for the generic drug to get market share. However, withdrawal of a product under those circumstances has resulted in antitrust claims, so product withdrawal must be carefully considered before implementation.

OVER-THE-COUNTER STRATEGY

Another strategy is to develop and launch an over-the-counter (OTC) version of the drug just prior to the time the original product's patent life expires, as done by Schering-Plough with Claritin and Astra Zeneca with Prilosec. This transfers a significant portion of the old prescription market to the new OTC market for the innovator and reduces market size for the generic company.

FDA CITIZEN'S PETITIONS

If there is a concern that the generic drug may be different in such a way that safety or effectiveness is called into question, another avenue is to make objections to the suitability of the generic product with the FDA by filing a Citizen's Petition (CP).

These are formal written requests to the FDA that the FDA is obliged to consider and reply to publicly. For example, Wyeth filed a CP on the suitability of an ANDA for its conjugated estrogen, Premarin. After lengthy deliberations, the FDA agreed with Wyeth and would not approve an ANDA for Premarin, based on its unique formulation that the company said could not be duplicated by a generic product. (Premarin is extracted from the urine of pregnant mares and is a natural hormone complex more like a biological and not readily duplicated chemically.)

Citizen's Petitions can be used to oppose generic ANDA filings based on a variety of bioequivalence challenges. Examples include identifying differences in metabolites, drug blood level peaks, food and alcohol effects or drug interactions that show that the generic does not act in the body the same way as the brand drug.

In response to complaints by the generic industry that Citizen's Petitions were being filed by branded drug companies for the purpose of delaying approval of ANDAs, legislation was enacted in late 2007 providing that FDA may not delay the approval of a pending ANDA or 505(b)(2) application as a result of a CP unless the FDA determines that the delay is necessary to protect public health. In addition, the FDA is authorized to deny any CP if it was submitted for the primary purpose of delaying approval of the ANDA if the CP does not raise valid scientific or regulatory issues. Finally the FDA must take action on the CP within 180 days from its submission. There is also language to prevent a CP from causing the loss of any part of the 180-day first-filer exclusivity from approval delays caused by a CP.

AUTHORIZED GENERICS

In an interesting turnabout, two major generic companies, Mylan Pharmaceuticals and Teva, filed CPs with the FDA some years ago to ban so-called "authorized generics". Authorized generics are generic products that an innovator company licenses to a third party during the 180-day first-filer generic exclusivity period, thereby effectively taking away the exclusivity period from the generic company that had it. The generic industry counts on the 180-day exclusivity period to make large profits and it is a key growth driver. The presence of a second generic product with lower prices effectively reduces their earnings. Though it is clear authorized generics benefit consumers with lower prices for drugs, the generic industry has been aggressive in trying to prevent them as they reduce generic company profits.

In 2004 the FDA denied the CPs and confirmed the rights of the innovator companies to sell authorized generic products indicating that the price reductions in the cost of generic drugs it provided were appropriate and in the public interest. Early examples of authorized generics include the well-known antidepressant Paxil (license granted to Par Pharmaceuticals by GlaxoSmithKline) and the oral contraceptive Ortho-Tricyclen (licensed by J&J to Watson Pharmaceuticals) though Barr Laboratories had first-filer exclusivity rights.

The launch of authorized generics has now become commonplace since that ruling. Subsequent litigation on the issue resulted in authorized generics being upheld by the courts. As a result, we are seeing more deals between innovators and certain generic companies for authorized generics. Turned away by the FDA and the Courts, the generic industry has also tried the political route. Various bills have been introduced since 2007 to ban authorized generics, but none have passed as of the end of 2013.

EXAMPLES OF LIFE-CYCLE MANAGEMENT

The following are two examples of life-cycle management. The first one illustrates the situation where the initial product has a good basic life-cycle plan built in from the beginning. The second example illustrates the case where no thought at all was given to life-cycle management before the initial product was approved. We will see that LCM can work well in both cases.

The Acular (ketorolac) Story

An innovative drug product, Toradol (ketorolac tromethamine), a non-steroidal anti-inflammatory drug (NSAID), was invented by Syntex (now part of Roche) in the early 1970s and was approved by FDA for systemic treatment of serious pain conditions. It is non-narcotic and non-habit forming and does not cause physical or mental dependence, as narcotics can. It is administered orally or by injection. Syntex filed and obtained patents on the new chemical entity, for its use in treatment of serious pain and on its method of manufacture.

Additional research begun in the late 1970s lead to the discovery that the compound also could be used topically in the treatment of certain eye conditions. A new patent was therefore filed for treatment of conditions of the eye with topical formulations containing ketorolac tromethamine. Syntex researchers then tried to formulate the compound into a commercially acceptable eye drop and ran into problems obtaining a robust, stable formulation. A number of Syntex formulation scientists worked for several years on the problem and eventually solved it through the use of a special stabilizer that had not previously been used for stabilizing ophthalmic pharmaceutical products. An additional patent was obtained on the ophthalmic formulation containing the new formulation with the new ophthalmic stabilizer.

The eye drop product was approved by FDA as Acular 0.5% and launched in 1992 and three patents were listed in the FDA Orange Book. The original 1995 patent expiration date of the compound patent was extended to 1997 by patent term extension. The expiration date for the ophthalmic use patent was 2002 and the expiration date of the formulation patent was 2009. Since the NCE patent had been extended, no further extensions could be made to the improvement patents. In addition, the FDA requested that a pediatric study be done and after its completion, the patent dates were effectively extended by six months.

The new ophthalmic formulation was entitled to a three-year FDA exclusivity for its new indication/new formulation for relief of ocular itching due to seasonal allergic conjunctivitis. After further clinical studies during the 1990s, the product was also approved in 1998 for an orphan condition, namely, inflammation following cataract surgery. This entitled the innovator to a seven-year FDA exclusivity to 2005, but only for that indication.

The Canadian based generic company Apotex filed an ANDA for Acular 0.5% in 2001 (for the first approved indi-

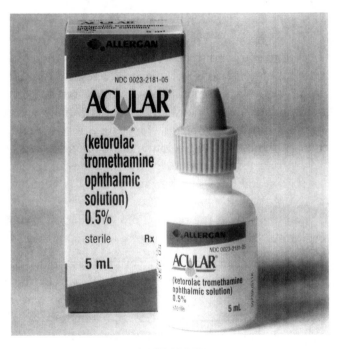

9. ACULAR 0.5%

cation only since the second indication was still protected by orphan designation) and sent a Paragraph IV certification asserting the formulation patent was invalid and not infringed. Within the 45-day period provided, a patent infringement suit was filed against Apotex and litigation commenced in the Federal District Court in San Francisco as a bench trial (without a jury) before U.S. District Court Judge Martin Jenkins. Under the terms of the Hatch Waxman Act, the FDA was not able to approve the ANDA for the product for up to 30 months from the date of notice of the Paragraph IV certification or until there was a Court decision concerning the patent.

The original 0.5% product tended to cause transient burning and stinging in the eye when it was used. To improve the product, Allergan, the company who had licensed Acular from Syntex, began developing a new formulation that used a lower concentration of the active drug, with the same effectiveness, and which was designed to be more comfortable to the patient. Patients testing the improved 0.4% reformulation reported less burning and stinging on installation of drops. In addition, the improved product was tested and approved for a new use, namely, reduction of ocular pain and burning and stinging following Lasik corneal surgery. The improvement was approved by FDA as Acular LS and the new product was launched in 2003.

Acular LS was listed in the Orange Book under the same formulation patent as the original product and received a three-year new use exclusivity based on the newly approved medical use. A short time thereafter, Apotex copied the improvement, filed an ANDA for it and sent a Paragraph IV notice. Apotex was sued within the 45-day period provided, and Acular LS likewise was litigated in the same court as the first product.

The multi-week trial on Acular 0.5% was completed by the summer of 2003 before the end of the 30-month period; however, the Court had not issued its ruling by the end of the 30-month

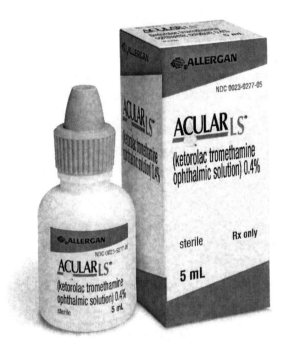

10. ACULAR LS 0.4%

period in October, 2003. On request of the company, the Court extended the 30-month period until the end of 2003, or until it issued its ruling, whichever came first.

The District Court ruled in December 2003 that the formulation patent was valid and infringed (*Syntex and Allergan v. Apotex*, 2003). Apotex subsequently appealed to the Federal Circuit which concluded in 2005 that the District Court had gotten it mostly right, but they remanded for issues having to do with the Court's fact findings on obviousness. In 2006, the District Court reconsidered its ruling in light of the views of the Federal Circuit and concluded its original decision was the correct one. The Federal Circuit affirmed that decision in 2007. Thereafter Apotex unsuccessfully requested the decision be reviewed by the Supreme Court.

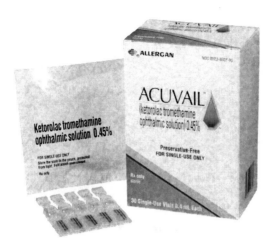

11. ACUVAIL (0.45%)

The case now being final, the FDA was instructed by the Court, in accordance with the provisions of the Hatch Waxman Act, not to approve the Apotex ANDA until expiration in 2009 of the final patent listed in the Orange Book and expiration of the pediatric extension six months after patent expiration.

The trial on Acular LS was handled by the same Court in 2007 by summary judgment, again upholding the patent just before the end of the second 30-month period and that decision was affirmed on appeal.

This example shows how the combination of good patent protection on each new invention (compound, second medical use and formulation), coupled with use of the Orange Book listing, patent term extension, an improvement to the product and four different FDA exclusivities (new use, new formulation, orphan and pediatric), have provided a reasonable life to the innovative eye care product and provided the public with new, innovative medicines for treatment of three important eye conditions. Note that the compound and ophthalmic use patents were never challenged. There were no further generic challenges after that. When the patents expired in late 2009, Apotex launched its generic versions. As a result of life-cycle management, the Acular product line had a 17 year life from 1992–2009.

As a post script, Allergan launched a new patented version of the product in July, 2009 called Acuvail (ketorolac 0.45%) in a preservative-free, unit dose formulation with carboxymethylcellulose for enhanced patient comfort, indicated for pain and inflammation following cataract surgery, so the product franchise still lives on until patent expiration in 2029.

The Alphagan (brimonidine) Story

Brimonidine was an alpha-2-adrenergic agonist drug compound thought to have therapeutic value in treating hypertension or elevated blood pressure. Warner-Lambert obtained US patent no. 3,890,319 on the compound in 1975 and worked on development, but the compound did not live up to its promise and development was cancelled by the mid-1980s and the scientific results were published.

Allergan scientists were at that time looking for new compounds to treat glaucoma, a condition of the eye characterized by

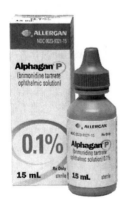
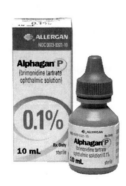
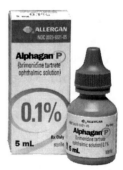

12. ALPHAGAN-P

elevated intraocular pressure. They thought brimonidine might work as a topical treatment for glaucoma and Allergan licensed the product from Warner-Lambert for development for ophthalmic use. When the compound was licensed, little thought was given to life-cycle management because at that time there were no ophthalmic generics and the general view in the industry was that generics were unlikely to be developed for specialized ophthalmic products.

The compound in the form of brimonidine tartrate (0.2%) was formulated and tested and ultimately approved by FDA in September, 1996 as a topical eye drop for the treatment of glaucoma. The company was happy to get the approval, but its proprietary position did not look good. By that time, ophthalmic generics were indeed upon the scene and the only compound patent had already expired in 1993. And there was no ophthalmic use patent, because that potential use had been previously disclosed in the Warner-Lambert publication and therefore it was too late to obtain such a patent on the ophthalmic use. And there was no formulation patent, as the formulation used in the development of the compound by Allergan was conventional. The only protection afforded the new drug was the five-year Hatch Waxman exclusivity, since the active compound, brimonidine tartrate, had never been previously approved, but that was still too short a time to justify the costs of development.

Better late than never, the company decided it needed to get to work on a life-cycle management program. It assembled a team of business, scientific, medical, technical and legal people who were charged with coming up with a strategy and practical plan to save the future of the product. After discussing the issues at some length, a basic plan was established to develop an improved version of the product which would be patented.

Over the next few years it was learned that some people were developing allergies to Alphagan 0.2% which were not serious, but caused red, itchy eyes in some patients and doctors were not happy with that. Allergan decided to develop an improvement which would reduce or eliminate that allergy problem.

A new 0.15% brimonidine tartrate formulation was developed using carboxymethylcellulose (CMC) as a solubility enhancer, and a proprietary preservative, stabilized chlorine dioxide, which the company had originally developed in the early 1990s for use with its line of contact lens care products. By reducing the concentration of brimonidine, while enhancing its solubility with CMC and a pH change, the new formulation was just as effective as the original formulation in decreasing intraocular pressure and it significantly reduced allergy affects due to the lowered concentration of the active drug. The new product, called Alphagan-P (0.15% brimonidine) was filed with FDA and approved in 2001 and launched immediately.

The patent attorneys were equally busy. They filed and obtained four new patents covering the new formulation, in addition to the existing patent covering the new preservative. Based on research work by company scientists, they filed and obtained two additional new patents claiming a method of protecting the optic nerve and a method of neural protection through the administration of brimonidine.

The two new method of use patents, U.S. Patents 6,194,415 and 6,248,741, were listed in the Orange Book in 2001 within 30 days of their issue dates, as provided under the Hatch Waxman Act. In addition, the company obtained approval from FDA to conduct pediatric studies and when those were completed and filed, the exclusivity period for Alphagan 0.2% was increased from five to 5.5 years.

However, the necessary patent listing in the Orange Book allowed Bausch & Lomb and Alcon to file ANDAs for Alphagan 0.2% before the end of the 5.5 year exclusivity period, since an ANDA may be filed after the end of the fourth year of exclusivity if a patent is listed in the Orange Book.

When Bausch & Lomb and Alcon filed their ANDAs for Alphagan 0.2% in 2001, they were required to file patent certifications to the patents listed in the Orange Book. Both filed paragraph IV certifications. As a result, the FDA would not be able to approve the ANDAs for 30 months from the date of the Paragraph IV notice.

Allergan initiated suit in the U.S. District Court for the Central District of California for inducement of patent infringement under 35 U.S.C. section 271(e)(2) within 45 days of receiving the paragraph IV notices. Both defendants filed motions for summary judgment arguing a claim of induced infringement was precluded under that statute, where the ANDA is for a use of the drug that is different from the use of the drug that is claimed in the asserted patent, i.e., a patent covering an off-label use. In 2002, the District Court agreed with generic defendants and so ordered.

On appeal in 2003, the Federal Circuit panel of three judges said that while they all personally believed Allergan was correct in listing an off-label patent in the Orange Book, a prior decision in a parallel case by another Federal Circuit panel only two months earlier (*Warner-Lambert v. Apotex*) had ruled that the listing of off-label patents was precluded by 271(e)(2), so they said they felt bound to follow the earlier ruling in favor of the generics. The FDA approved the ANDAs the next day. (As an historical aside, that ruling was codified by Congress in the December, 2003 Medicare Act Amendments.)

However, this turned out to be a pyrrhic victory for B&L and Alcon as Alphagan-P (0.15%) had become a very successful improvement product. In the two years since it was launched, virtually the entire market for the drug had moved from the earlier 0.2% version to the improved 0.15% product. When Alcon and B&L launched their generic copies of the earlier 0.2% version soon thereafter, there was virtually no market for them and sales of Alphagan-P (0.15%) continued to grow to over $350 million annually by 2009.

Of course, as Yogi Berra famously said, "it ain't over 'til it's over". Alcon apparently was not pleased with the result of copying the original product, so it set out to compete with the improvement by attempting to design around Allergan's product patents and develop its own ophthalmic formulation of 0.15% brimonidine. After completing its development including clinical trials, Alcon filed a 505(b)(2) application for its own version of 0.15% brimonidine ophthalmic in 2004. The formulation was similar to Alphagan-P (0.15% brimonidine), but used a different preservative and replaced the CMC with other ingredients.

Alcon was again required to make a Paragraph IV certification and Allergan filed suit in Delaware on two of the five patents, the '337 and '834 patents, since Allergan concluded the other three patents did not cover Alcon's new formulation. Alcon received tentative approval from FDA in 2005, but the 30-month stay prevented the FDA from granting final approval.

As that first lawsuit was pending, Allergan did an interesting thing. It filed a second patent infringement case against Alcon on one of Alcon's important products, Vigamox, Alcon's leading ophthalmic ocular antibiotic, based on two patents owned by Allergan: 6,166,012 and 6,492,361 directed to self-preserved antibiotic products.

Shortly thereafter both suits were settled by Allergan agreeing to withdraw its antibiotic infringement suit and Alcon agreeing to accept a royalty bearing license under Allergan's brimonidine patents starting late 2009. (A good example of how having some patents potentially covering a competitor's product, but held in reserve, may come in handy someday.)

One reason Allergan was willing to license Alcon on its flagship Alphagan-P product starting in late 2009 was that Allergan had also been working on a further improvement of Alphagan-P. Allergan was able to adjust the formulation again such that it could lower the concentration of brimonidine to 0.1% without loss of efficacy. The new product called

Alphagan-P (0.1%) was approved by FDA in early 2005 and was launched soon thereafter.

In early 2007 Apotex, a large Canadian generic company, and Exela, a small Indian drug development company, each filed ANDAs for Alphagan-P for both the 0.15% and 0.1% strengths. Apotex copied the formula more or less exactly and was sued on all five patents. Exela tried to design around the Allergan formulation and was sued on only the '834 patent. Both cases were consolidated in Delaware. In 2009, after a full trial on the merits, Chief Judge Gregory M. Sleet of the U.S. District Court for Delaware, in a 43 page opinion, held all of Allergan's patents valid and infringed and directed the FDA not to approve their generic versions of Alphagan-P until the last patent to expire in 2022.

On appeal, in *In re Brimonidine Patent Litigation* (Fed. Cir. 2011), the Federal Circuit, with one judge dissenting in part, reversed the District Court as to only one of the patents and upheld the other 4 patents after finding one claim valid and infringed. As a result, the FDA was ordered not to approve the Apotex generic product until the last to expire of the 4 patents in 2022.

Though the Court also found that Exela's new formulation did not infringe the '834 patent, it was sufficiently different from the Allergan product formulation that Exela was not able to obtain FDA approval of its formulation without performing bioequivalence studies to demonstrate its new formula was bioequivalent to Allergan's product. Exela declined to do the studies, so its ANDA was never approved.

This is a good example of why narrow formulation claims are useful. While Exela's design-around formulation was sufficiently different to avoid the narrow patent claims, that same difference lead to an expensive bioequivalence study being required by FDA for approval and a small generic company like Exela was not able or willing to do it.

Combigan

What may perhaps be the final chapter of the Alphagan saga began in the Eastern District of Texas, the well-known Marshall division. It seems Allergan developed one more brimonidine improvement by being the first to develop a combination product of brimonidine with timolol, a drug previously used to treat glaucoma. Doctors seem to like the new combination, called Combigan. It was approved and launched in 2007.

While the combination product was doing well commercially, it was a fact that both compounds were well known glaucoma agents used individually and even had been previously prescribed concomitantly, though they had never before existed together in one bottle. It was also known that to be effective, brimondine was dosed 3 times a day while timolol only needed to be dosed 2 times a day. It was discovered that one of the unexpected benefits of the combination was that one could reduce the number of daily doses of brimonidine from 3 to 2 without loss of efficacy by combining it with timolol. As a result, Allergan received four patents on Combigan: two covering the composition (7,323,463 and 7,642,258), one covering the method of treatment (7,320,976) and one covering the unexpected discovery on daily dosage (7,030,149) and listed them in the Orange Book.

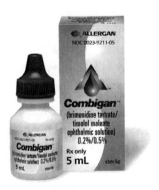

13. COMBIGAN

In 2008 two generic companies, Sandoz and Hi-Tech Pharmacal, filed ANDAs seeking approval of generic Combigan. In 2009 the two resulting Hatch Waxman cases were consolidated in Marshall, Texas. The District Court found the four patents to be valid and infringed. On appeal, in *Allergan v. Sandoz* (Fed. Cir. 2013), all three judges on the panel of the Federal Circuit found the claims of one of the patents directed to the combination invalid, but two of the three judges found claim 4 of the '149 patent directed to the unexpected discovery that the dosage could be reduced from 3x/day to 2x/day valid and infringed. The Court concluded that:

> *"The '258, '976 and '149 patents each expire on April 19th, 2022. Because we conclude that claim 4 of the '149 patent is [valid and infringed] the Appellants (Sandoz and Hi-Tech) will be unable to enter the market until that date. Accordingly, we find it unnecessary to address the claims of the '258 and '976 patents."*

This was indeed a close case, with the Court finding one of the patents covering the composition invalid, but upholding the validity of one claim of one of the other three patents covering the unexpected discovery on dosage and that by only a 2 to 1 majority. Interestingly, the Court declined to review the other two patents saying that finding one claim of one patent being valid was sufficient since all of the patents expired the same day.

As a result, a single product, with no patents and a 5.5 year FDA regulatory exclusivity launched in 1996, was converted to a multi-product *franchise* of four products developed over an 11 year period, covered by nine patents and multiple 3 year marketing exclusivities and maintained during multiple patent litigations, ultimately resulting in significant on-going branded sales expected through 2022.

The ALPHAGAN story dramatically illustrates and proves the power of life-cycle management. One can start with a product having limited exclusivity and no patent protection; and with a concerted effort of many talented and creative people working on life-cycle management, convert that short lived product into a successful, long term product franchise that provides effective and improved therapies to the public and sales and profits to the company over many years.

The foregoing examples illustrate the interactive, multifaceted nature of life-cycle management through integration of patents, FDA regulatory exclusivity, knowledge of FDA regulatory procedures, serial product improvements and equally important, a creative patent origination group and an equally talented patent enforcement team. A good life-cycle management program uses all of its parts in parallel for effectiveness and for redundancy, so that failure of any one part will not necessarily result in a short product life.

Congratulations. All of you are now experts in pharmaceutical product life-cycle management, or certainly compared to the average person, well informed on the subject. While I have tried to keep the explanation of the subject light and hopefully interesting, it is a serious matter which affects the lives of millions for better or worse.

Chapter 9

Conclusions and Final Thoughts

The following are some ideas to improve the two main problems I see with fostering and maintaining an ongoing, thriving and innovative pharmaceutical industry: consumer and political backlash to the perception/reality of excessive prices being charged to U.S. consumers for current brand-name medicines; and diminishing incentives to the innovative pharma industry to develop vital new future medicines.

DRUG POLICY V. INDUSTRIAL POLICY

When one talks about policy matters with drugs, the tendency is to limit the discussion to the need to provide high quality, low cost drugs to the public. What is often not discussed is the value to the public of a thriving research-based innovative pharmaceutical and biotech industry that employs millions of people in the U.S. including doctors, scientists, engineers, researchers, managers, accountants, salesman, secretaries, factory workers and even lawyers in well-paying jobs. While Canada has low-priced drugs, it has no innovative pharma industry and you would be surprised how many talented Canadians must come to the U.S. to work for American pharmaceutical companies for that reason.

And of course it is a truism that today's newly discovered, though admittedly expensive, innovative drugs become tomorrow's inexpensive generics. No new discoveries today, no new generics tomorrow. So I believe it is in our collective best interests to support America's innovative pharma industry today, so we can continue to have a thriving pharma industry as well as inexpensive generics tomorrow.

LONGER EXCLUSIVITY TERMS

Newly discovered conventional drugs in the U.S. today are entitled to only 5.5 years of marketing exclusivity before generics can freely copy them in the absence of a patent, based on a law passed 30 years ago, when drug discovery and development costs and regulatory requirements for approval were far less than today. That guaranteed time is too short for a reasonable return on the large investment in time and money now required to develop and obtain approval for a new drug. While patents may add to that life, they are not a sure thing and the risk reward equation often tilts against development of the most promising drugs for the reason the patents on them are not so promising. That is a terrible reason for not developing a promising life-saving medicine, but that is the reality.

The exclusivity term in the U.S. for new conventional drugs should be doubled to terms like the new European regulatory exclusivity of 10–12 years or the newly legislated 12.5 years of regulatory exclusivity for approved biologics or the 10.5 years for an FDA designated Qualified Infective Disease Product (QIDP) or 12.5 years for an Orphan QIDP. That alone would be sufficient to encourage the development of new and innovative future medicines that had less than needed patent coverage, which otherwise would not be commercially developed without more certainty on an adequate commercial life of the product for the developer.

UNIFORM INTERNATIONAL APPROVAL STANDARDS

Another complex issue is drug costs and the long times for development. People believe drug costs are too high and that innovative pharmaceutical companies are making too much money. One of the ways to lower drug costs would be to have more cooperation between governmental drug regulatory agencies around the world. At the present time, with limited exceptions, new drugs must be approved, re-approved and re-approved again in each country or region. The tests necessary to obtain drug approval in the U.S. will not get the same drug approved in Europe or Japan and vice versa. Companies have to spend hundreds of millions of dollars testing and retesting new drugs to satisfy each country's particular requirements. At one time in the past, Japan even required pre-clinical testing to be re-done on Japanese rats!

Thus drug testing requirements have many of the attributes of non-tariff barriers to competition. Japan protects its domestic pharmaceutical industry in this way as does the U.S. and Europe. If the major world governments' health authorities would cooperate on *uniform approval requirements*, new drug prices could be lower because development costs would be significantly reduced and people all over the world would have much faster access to new and better medicines.

PRICE CONTROLS AND "FREE RIDE" ISSUES

Another issue concerning the high cost of new drugs is drug price controls in some countries. These countries control the price of drugs to keep prices low for their citizens, but it only works because there are enough countries that either do not control prices or allow sufficiently high prices so that innovative drug developers can still profitably develop new drugs. This results in a "free ride" for the citizens of the low-priced countries because the drugs could not be developed for the prices allowed; and it is available to them only because other countries allow sufficiently high prices that justify the development costs and risks.

That is why Americans were calling for drug re-importation from Canada, where they see the same drugs that they buy in the U.S. cost less in Canada. That's because Canada has drug price controls and the U.S. generally does not, though there are required discounts and rebates for Medicare and state drug programs like Medicaid. However, instead of getting mad at Canada for controlling drug prices, they get mad at the drug companies for what they perceive as price gouging. If those same drug price controls were in effect in the U.S., the drugs in question may not have been developed in the first place, and then there would be nothing to be mad about (except the absence of the new and better drug.) On the other hand, with 80% of prescriptions now being generic, perhaps the focus on pricing for the other 20% is somewhat misplaced.

PRESCRIBING GENERIC DRUGS EVEN MORE OFTEN

Another way overall drug prices could be kept lower in America is if doctors would prescribe generic drugs even more often. Drug companies promote their latest and greatest new generation of drug products that are typically more expensive than the comparable product they previously promoted and sold; especially if the product has now become a generic. These once new drugs did not suddenly become old, inadequate drugs overnight. Even though some of the latest drugs may offer improvements over the older drugs, there may not be a significant difference for others and new drugs may have yet undiscovered side effects which old drugs do not.

For example one of the best proton pump inhibitors ever invented for reducing stomach acid was Prilosec (omeprazole), which was invented, developed and sold by Astra Zeneca. At one time, it was the world's leading drug in terms of sales. The patents on Prilosec have expired and the product has become generic and OTC. As part of Astra Zeneca's product life-cycle management plan, it developed and is currently very successfully marketing, as a new product, one of the chemical isomers that make up omeprazole called Nexium. Nexium may have some benefits over Prilosec, but for many Prilosec would work just as well as Nexium and at a much lower cost. Yet Nexium's sales continue to grow. This is a good example of how doctors could lower medicine costs for patients by recommending lower cost Prilosec OTC or prescribing the generic of Prilosec (omeprazole) instead of prescribing Nexium.

Of course this is more complicated than it first appears. People and insurance plans can complicate things. Some patients may prefer Nexium because they get prescription drugs at low cost through their insurance plans. If they had to buy Prilosec OTC, it would cost them more since insurance won't cover OTC products. And you might not be very happy with your GI specialist if he charged you $250 for telling you to use an OTC medication you could have purchased without seeing him.

However, where there is no specific need for the latest and likely more expensive drug, doctors should prescribe the older, more reliable and probably safer drugs that are likely to have become generic. For example, the older anti-inflammatory drug ibuprofen (Advil) and the latest one, Vioxx, are similarly acting drugs, but Vioxx turned out to have potential serious safety issues for long-term use and was withdrawn from the market. And while we complain about the cost of new drugs, we generally don't insist our physicians offer us older, less expensive and possibly safer alternatives and our health insurers don't give us much incentive to do so either. We shop for most things, but typically not for drugs. Could it be dear Brutus, that the fault lies not in our stars, but in ourselves?

As a closing thought, the innovative pharmaceutical industry, for all its faults, remains a consummate life-affirming and life-enhancing industry. For ourselves, and especially for our posterity, I believe no effort should be spared to ensure that the innovative pharmaceutical industry continues to survive and prosper. After all, the life they save may be your own.

GLOSSARY OF TERMS

510K – A form of filing with FDA for approval of a medical device that refers to an existing approval of a similar medical device.

505(b)(2) – A form of filing with FDA for a drug that refers to published data for safety and efficacy which also may be used in place of an ANDA for copying an approved drug with changes in the drug formulation or NCE.

Active moiety – The biologically active portion of a drug molecule which provides the pharmacological activity of the drug.

AIA – America Invents Act, converting the U.S. to a first-to-file country from first-to-invent, effective March 16, 2013.

ANDA – Abbreviated New Drug Application: the FDA filing for a generic drug approval.

Authorized generic – A generic version of a branded drug commercialized by the owner of the corresponding brand name drug itself or through a designated third party.

Bioequivalence – A determination by FDA that a generic drug product is bioequivalent to the branded reference drug is part of the requirement for determining therapeutic equivalence.

A finding of bioequivalence requires that the generic drug product must be shown to act in the body in the same or substantially similar way as the branded drug product. Typically, bioequivalence is established by showing comparable blood levels of active drug substance produced by the generic product and the brand name product. Limited waivers for establishing bioequivalence are available for certain classes of drug products such as topical ophthalmic (eye) and otic (ear) solutions.

Biological product – A drug product generally derived from living material—human, animal or microorganism—that is complex in structure and usually not fully characterized, such as gene-based and cellular biologics, often produced by biotechnology methods.

Biogeneric – A generic of a biological drug; also known as a follow-on biologic or biosimilar.

Biosimilar – The term used for a "similar biological medicinal product," for a generic of a biological drug.

BLA – Biological License Application: the FDA filing for approval of a biologic.

Brand name drug – A drug marketed under a proprietary, trademark-protected name.

CAFC – Court of Appeals for the Federal Circuit. This is the only court of appeals that hears all patent appeals from the Federal District Courts and the International Trade Commission.

CBER – Center for Biologics Evaluation and Research, a division of FDA.

CDER – Center for Drug Evaluation and Research, a division of FDA.

Centralized procedure – An administrative procedure in Europe for approving new drugs in all European Union (EU) countries by a single review.

Certificate of Free Sale – A document which smaller countries require to permit sales of a prescription drug in that country, establishing that the drug is on sale in a larger country such as the U.S. and thus has been found to be safe and effective.

Certificate of Pharmaceutical Product – A new name for a Certificate of Free Sale.

cGLP – Current Good Laboratory Practices.

cGMP – Current Good Manufacturing Practices.

CIP – Continuation-in-part: a type of continuation of a patent application which makes changes in an existing patent application and obtains the benefit of its filing date for the non-changed portion.

Citizen's Petition – A formal written request to FDA requesting an administrative action ruling. Sometimes used by brand name companies to point out defects in or lack of bioequivalence of generic drug products. Also used by generic companies to attempt to resolve conflicting first-filer rights, i.e., 180-day exclusivity issues.

Claims – Numbered paragraphs at the end of a patent which are the most important part of a patent and define the scope of a patented invention as a deed to real property describes the property lines of the real property.

Compound patent – A form of patent that claims a compound and is generally the most preferred type of patent claim covering a pharmaceutical product.

CON – Continuation: a type of patent application that is the same as a predecessor patent application and retains its filing date.

Constructive reduction to practice – The filing of a patent application in the U.S. is the legal equivalent to having reduced the invention to practice.

CP – Citizen's Petition: a form of request to FDA concerning drug products including exclusivity issues.

Data exclusivity – A period of regulatory exclusivity during which a regulatory agency will not accept an application for a generic drug.

DDMAC – Division for Drug Marketing, Advertising and Communications, a former name for a division of FDA now called Office of Prescription Drug Promotion.

Declaratory judgment – A request to a court to make a legal determination concerning a party's rights or obligations, e.g., under a contract. Also used by a party to obtain a ruling that a patent is invalid or to obtain a ruling of non-infringement.

Dependent claim – A form of patent claim that internally references another claim for part of its content.

DJ – Declaratory judgment.

DMF – Drug Master File.

Doctrine of Equivalents – Non-literal infringement of a patent where it is determined there are insubstantial differences between a patent claim and the infringing product or process.

Dosage form – The physical form in which a drug is produced and dispensed, such as a tablet, capsule or injectable.

Drug – A drug is defined as:

- a substance recognized by an official pharmacopoeia or formulary
- a substance intended for use in the diagnosis, cure, mitigation, treatment or prevention of disease
- a substance (other than food) intended to affect the structure or any function of the body
- a substance intended for use as a component of a medicine
- biological products are included within this definition and are generally covered by the same laws and regulations

Drug product – The finished dosage form that contains a drug substance, usually in association with other active or inactive ingredients.

EMA – European Medicines Agency.

EPO – European Patent Office.

Equivalents – See Doctrine of Equivalents.

Established name – The formal name given to each drug substance or NCE; commonly known as the generic name.

FDA – U.S. Food and Drug Administration.

FDASIA – FDA Safety and Innovation Act

Federal District Courts – The U.S. Federal Courts that hear patent infringement cases.

First-Filer – The informal designation given to a generic company that is the first in time to file an acceptable ANDA for a patented branded drug product with a Paragraph IV certification, which makes it eligible for the 180-day exclusivity provided by the Hatch Waxman Act. More than one generic company can obtain first-filer status for the same drug.

Formulation patent – A type of patent designed to cover a drug formulation and typically is the narrowest of patents covering drugs products.

Generic drug – A drug product that is a copy of a brand-name drug and is approved for sale based on safety and efficacy data developed by the brand drug owner. It may be substituted at the pharmacy level for the brand name drug without a doctor's approval if it is "A" rated by FDA, but not if it is "B" rated.

Grace Period – A period of time in which a U.S. inventor may file a patent after disclosure of his invention without loss of rights—typically one year.

GLP – Good Laboratory Practices.

GMP – Good Manufacturing Practices.

Hatch Waxman Act – The common name of the federal law establishing generic drugs and patent term extensions, officially known as the "Drug Price Competition and Patent Term Restoration Act of 1984".

IDE – Investigational Device Exemption: the first filing with FDA for approval to test a Class III medical device in humans.

IND – Investigational New Drug: the first filing with FDA for approval to test a new drug in humans.

Independent claim – A form of patent claim that does not make any reference to another claim.

Inducement of infringement – A type of indirect infringement of a patent in which the infringer induces a third party to directly infringe the patent. It can be asserted against a manufacturer of a generic drug product with labelling for a medical use covered by a patent.

Infringement – The act of violating the claims of a valid and enforceable patent.

Infringement opinion – A formal legal opinion on whether a product or process infringes a patent and often obtained prior to litigation by a potential infringer for reliance to avoid a charge of willful infringement.

Interference – A U.S. Patent Office administrative procedure to establish who is the first inventor of a given invention when two or more inventors claim the same invention at about the same time.

Label – The FDA approved label is the official description of a drug product which includes its indication (what the drug is used for), who should take it, adverse events (side effects), instructions for use in pregnancy, children and other populations, and safety information for the patient.

Life-Cycle Management – A strategy for extending the useful life of branded medical products, especially pharmaceutical and biologic products.

MAA – Marketing Authorization Application: the term used in the European Union for the form of filing for an approved drug (corresponds to a New Drug Application (NDA) in the U.S.)

Marketing exclusivity – A period of regulatory exclusivity during which a regulatory agency will not approve a generic application for marketing a drug.

MRP – Mutual Recognition Procedure.

Medical use patent – A type of patent covering the medical use of a drug product; typically, the second best form of patent protection for a pharmaceutical product, between compound patents and formulation patents.

Mutual Recognition Procedure – An administrative procedure for approving new drugs in the European Union one country at a time.

NCE – New chemical entity

NME – New molecular entity: Same as new chemical entity, but broadened to include new biologics.

NDA – New Drug Application: the FDA filing for approval of a new drug. The application contains data including chemistry, pharmacology, medical, biopharmaceutical and statistics.

New chemical entity – The name given to a chemical compound that is being approved for the first time in a given country in a drug product. Also called new molecular entity (NME).

NHI – A Japan agency that provides reimbursement prices for approved drugs in Japan.

Non-obvious – One of the requirements for patentability.

Novel – One of the requirements for patentability.

Off-label use – The use of an approved drug product by doctors to treat a specific disease or condition not approved by FDA for that drug.

OGD – Office of Generic Drugs: a division of FDA responsible for approving generic drugs.

OPDP – Office of Prescription Drug Promotion.

Orange Book – The informal name given to the FDA publication "Approved Drug Products and Therapeutic Equivalents". The Orange Book is a website where the FDA lists approved drugs and related patent and regulatory exclusivities.

Orphan drug – A designation given by FDA for a drug or biologic product that meets certain criteria including that there are less than 200,000 persons in the U.S. having the disease or condition to be treated. Also available in Europe and Japan.

OTC – Over-the-counter: a designation for a drug product that does not require a prescription.

Paper NDA – A filing for drug approval under section 505(b)(2) of the FDA regulations; typically used for filing of a generic product with one or more changes to a branded drug product formulation.

Paragraph IV certification – A certification provided by a generic company to a brand drug NDA owner and patent owner that states that a patent listed in the Orange Book for the drug product is either invalid or not infringed.

Parallel trade – Importation and sale of a branded drug in a second country, by a third party not related to the drug product owner, following authorized sale by the drug owner in another country. Also called parallel imports.

Patent Examiner – An employee of a national Patent Office who examines patents for approval.

Patent Office – A governmental agency responsible for granting and administering patents.

Patent prosecution – Written correspondence between the patent owner or his attorney and the patent examiner assigned to examine the patent owner's patent application concerning the patentability of the invention submitted.

PDMA – Prescription Drug Marketing Act of 1988.

PDUFA – Prescription Drug Marketing User Fee Act of 1992 that requires drug and biologic drug filers to pay fees to FDA for evaluation of their respective NDAs and BLAs.

PDUFA Date – The date the FDA is required to complete its first review of an NDA; generally ten months following acceptance for filing by FDA or six months with expedited review.

Pediatric exclusivity – An additional six-month period of exclusivity for a drug listed in the Orange Book that has met certain requirements for testing in children.

Pharmaceutical equivalents – Part of the requirement for generics to be therapeutically equivalent. FDA considers drug products to be pharmaceutical equivalents if they meet the following criteria:

- they contain the same active ingredients(s)

- they have the same dosage form and route of administration

- they are identical in strength or concentration

Pharmaceutical equivalent drug products may differ in other characteristics such as formulation excipients (e.g., color, flavor, etc.), shape, scoring and to some extent labelling.

Phase I – First study of a new drug in a small number of healthy human patients to establish safety.

Phase II – The second study of a new drug in a moderate number of human patients having the disease or condition to be treated to establish efficacy and dose ranging.

Phase III – The third study of a new drug in a large number of human patients to establish safety and efficacy.

Phase IV – Post-marketing studies to further establish safety.

PMA – Pre-marketing approval filing with FDA for a Class III medical device. Corresponds to an NDA for pharmaceuticals or a BLA for biologicals.

Polymorphs – Different physical forms of the same active drug, such as different crystalline forms, different hydrates, solvates or amorphous forms.

Prescription drug product – A drug product requiring a doctor's authorization to purchase.

Prior art – Publications or patents dated prior to the date of invention or prior to the patent filing date and which disclose or suggest the claimed invention, subject to any legally available "grace period".

Proprietary name – The name given to a drug product by the owner. Commonly called the brand name.

Prosecution history estoppel – A legal concept that limits the application of the doctrine of equivalents based on statements or narrowing amendments made to the claims during the prosecution of a patent application before the U.S. Patent Office.

PTO – U.S. Patent and Trademark Office

QIDP – Qualified Infectious Disease Product.

Qualified Infectious Disease Product – an antimicrobial drug for treating pathogens which pose a serious threat to public health. If so designated by FDA, an approved QIDP is entitled to 5 additional years of marketing exclusivity and an NCE QIDP is also entitled to 5 years additional data exclusivity.

Reference drug – The brand name drug intended to be copied by a generic drug through the filing of an ANDA.

RMS – Reference Member State. The name of the country in the European Union that is the initial country used for the Mutual Recognition Procedure for drug approval.

Submarine patent – A patent that has been pending for a long time in secrecy and which then issues with claims for inventions after those inventions have been incorporated in well-established products.

Tentative approval – Approval of a generic drug before the expiration of any patents or exclusivity accorded to the branded or reference drug. The FDA delays final approval until all patent or exclusivity issues have been resolved. A tentative approval does not allow the applicant to market the generic product.

Therapeutic equivalents – Generic drug products are classified as therapeutically equivalent if they are both pharmaceutically equivalent and bioequivalent. Generic drug products that are therapeutically equivalent can be substituted at the pharmacy for a branded drug product without approval of the doctor, and require the following:

- They must be pharmaceutical equivalents (contain the same active ingredient(s), dosage form, route of administration and strength).

- FDA assigns a therapeutic equivalence code or rating of "A" meaning the FDA has determined the generic drug product is therapeutically equivalent to the branded drug product and there is no *in vivo* bioequivalence issue known or suspected.

- Those products which the FDA determines are not therapeutic equivalents are assigned a "B" code or rating.

- Generic drugs which are not "A" rated cannot be substituted for the brand name drug at the pharmacy without a doctor's authorization.

- Therapeutically equivalent oral drug products are rated "AB" and therapeutically equivalent topical drugs are rated "AT".

Validity opinion – A formal legal opinion on the validity of a patent often obtained by a potential infringer as a defense to a claim of willful infringement.

Willful infringement – A finding by a Court that a party found to have infringed a patent did so intentionally, allowing any damage award to be increased by as much as three times at the discretion of the judge.

CPSIA information can be obtained at www.ICGtesting.com
Printed in the USA
LVOW12s0257170514

386085LV00003B/254/P